TOOLS FOR STRUCTURED DESIGN

Marilyn Bohl

TOOLS FOR STRUCTURED DESIGN

SCIENCE RESEARCH ASSOCIATES, INC.
Chicago, Henley-on-Thames, Sydney, Toronto

A Subsidiary of IBM

Compositor	Reprographex
Acquisition Editor	Robert L. Safran
Project Editor	Jay Schauer
Text Design	Staff
Cover Design	Don Fujimoto

Library of Congress Cataloging in Publication Data

Bohl, Marilyn.
 Tools for structured design.

 1. Structured programming. I. Title.
QA76.6.B63   001.6′425   77-13704
ISBN 0-574-21170-5

10 9 8 7

PREFACE

This book is intended for systems designers and programmers. Because of its tutorial nature, it is particularly useful to persons who are studying in these areas. While some background in systems design or programming may be helpful to the reader, neither is required or assumed.

There are five basic steps in computer program development:

- Defining the problem to be solved
- Developing a solution algorithm
- Expressing the algorithm in programming language
- Verifying the program
- Completing all required documentation

In this book, we look first at the basic concept of an algorithm—what an algorithm is, and why one is needed, both in computer-program development and in our daily lives. Then we look at how we develop an algorithm. Our objective is to analyze a problem and express its solution in such a way that the computer can be directed to follow the problem-solving procedure.

With simple language and many examples, this book shows how to understand and use many important problem-solving tools. We start with system and program flowcharts. The flowcharting guidelines approved and published by the American National Standards Institute (ANSI) and its international counterpart, the International Standards Organization (ISO), are explained and applied in solution planning. Emphasis is placed on maintaining an overall structure in program design. We show how to use pseudocode as an alternative or supplement to flowcharting in planning the logic of a well-structured program.

The concept of structure can be applied to system as well as program design. So we look next at techniques of top-down, modular system and program development. We show how to read and develop structure charts showing the hierarchical relationships of the programs, or modules, within a system. We study Hierarchy-Input-Process-Output (HIPO) diagrams an another means of picturing the structure within a system, and the inputs, processing, and outputs of its component parts.

Upon completion, the solution algorithm, or system and program design, can and should be verified. We suggest some techniques for doing so in this book. The purpose of verification is to detect and eliminate errors as early in program development as possible. Design documentation in flowchart, pseudocode, or other design-language form is also useful in subsequent program coding and program checkout. Creating the necessary documentation is not a burdensome final task of program development because much of it is created as an integral part of the program-development process.

ANSI-approved symbols for system flowcharting are pictured and explained briefly, with examples, in Appendix A of this book. ANSI-approved symbols for program flowcharting are presented in Appendix B. The basic control patterns of structured programming are summarized in Appendix C. These appendixes should be referred to whenever you are in doubt about which symbols to use on flowcharts.

Sample problems are included throughout these lessons to show the use of program-design tools in practical situations. A variety of exercises are given at the end of each lesson to help you apply what you have learned. Responses to selected exercises are provided in Appendix D so that you can evaluate your understanding of the material.

If this book is used as a class supplement, the instructor may not require you to do all the exercises. If you are using the book in relation to class work or in self-study, you should work as many as you can. They are a good way to check your progress.

This book expands upon *Flowcharting Techniques,* a widely used earlier reference by this author. As indicated before, this new book incorporates the system and program flowcharting techniques applied in that earlier text; in addition, more recently introduced design tools are described and applied in problem solving.

Marilyn Bohl

CONTENTS

DEVELOPING AN ALGORITHM

A computer is an extremely powerful, fast machine. In less than a second, it can perform difficult calculations that otherwise would take days, months, or years to perform. Yet a computer has no magical power; it is only a tool. It cannot devise a plan or decide to act. It can do only what it is told, in exactly the way it is told. A computer is only as effective as the set of instructions that control it. The set of instructions is called an **algorithm**, a **procedure**, or a **program**.

The term *algorithm* may be new to you, but most of us use numerous algorithms daily. For example, we adopt routine procedures, or algorithms, for getting up in the morning, fixing meals, going to work, and so on. One task required more often than some of us like—especially when an important game is being televised—is getting a haircut. A typical algorithm for such a situation is shown in Figure 1-1.

Figure 1-1 is an example of a **flowchart**, **block diagram**, or **logic diagram**. Although we have not discussed flowcharts yet, you can probably follow the flowlines in the example. The diamonds are decision symbols, points where alternate paths may be taken. The circles are connector symbols, directing you to matching connector symbols elsewhere on the flowchart.

In common practice, the algorithm shown in Figure 1-1 is carried out somewhat informally. The person who executes the algorithm may even be unaware of following an algorithm. In other situations, however, algorithms are often more formally defined. Business operations within a company are firmly established, for example. Uniform accounting procedures must be followed, inventory must be tightly controlled, manufacturing volumes must be correlated with both distribution and sales, and so on.

Consider the sales operations of a large department store. A sales manager delegates responsibilities to supervisors in various departments. Each supervisor submits a weekly sales report that is checked against inventory changes and then used as the basis for figuring commissions for department employees. Here is a task, or problem,

1

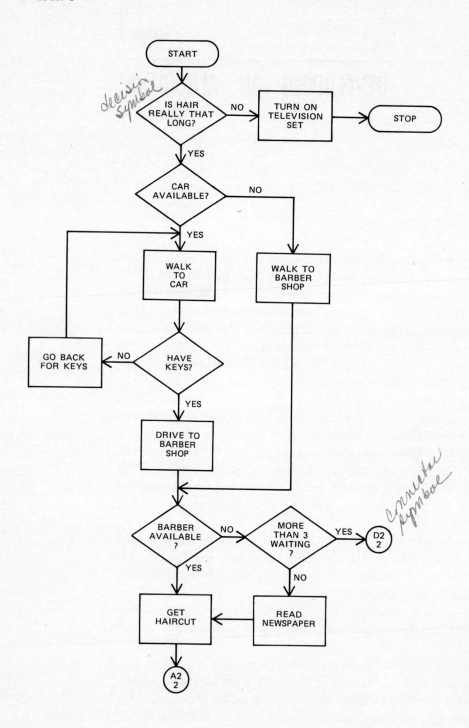

Figure 1-1

that confronts each supervisor: how to prepare the weekly sales report for his or her department. In some stores, each supervisor may be asked to develop his or her own procedure. In other stores, the sales manager develops a detailed set of instructions for each supervisor. In either case, one starts with the sales data available to

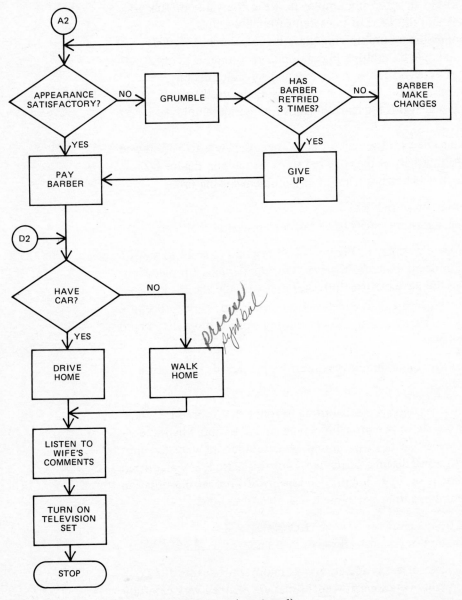

Figure 1-1 (continued)

the supervisor, thinks about the weekly sales report that is needed, and plans how to prepare the report on the basis of the sales data.

Here is a representative set of instructions for the supervisor of the large appliances department:

1. Select the weekly sales totals for any employee. Read the value of full price items from column A and the value of sales items from column B.
2. Compute the A commission by multiplying the value in column A by 6%.
3. Compute the B commission by multiplying the value in column B by 3%.
4. Compute the total pay due: $50.00 + A commission + B commission.
5. Enter the total pay opposite the employee's name in the payroll ledger.
6. Return to step 1 and repeat this sequence of steps for another employee.

These instructions can also be expressed pictorially. Then, the steps to be followed can be seen at a glance. A flowchart of the required steps is shown in Figure 1-2.

We have just traced the first two major parts of any problem-solving task:

- defining the problem to be solved, and
- developing a solution algorithm—steps to be taken to solve the problem.

The first five steps on the flowchart in Figure 1-2 correspond exactly to steps 1 through 5 of the written procedure. Note, however, that the flowchart provides for a situation not accounted for in the written procedure: eventually the weekly sales totals for all employees in the department will have been processed, so the procedure need not be executed again. Flowcharting the procedure helps us to see that step 6 should be rewritten as follows:

6. If weekly sales totals for more employees must be processed, then return to step 1; otherwise, stop.

Without this modification, the supervisor attempting to follow the procedure would have no instruction to stop. He or she probably would decide to quit when weekly sales totals for all employees had been processed. A computer, however, cannot act independently; it has no intelligence of its own. For this reason, any algorithm that we use to direct it must be set up to identify all aspects of a processing situation and to present, in detail, all steps to be performed. The algorithm must:

- use only operations from a given set of basic operations, and
- produce the problem solution, or answer, in a finite number of such operations.

The concept of a "given set of basic operations" is important because the computer can perform only certain operations; its capabilities are planned very carefully by **hardware** designers who lay out specifications that direct subsequent construction of the machine. The concept of a "finite number of such operations" is important because each operation performed by a computer takes a certain amount of

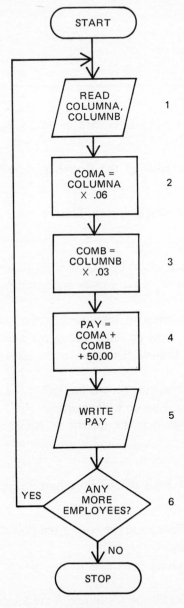

Figure 1-2

time (typically, about one-millionth of a second, or less). If an unlimited number of steps is required, it is not possible, even using the computer, to obtain the solution in a finite amount of time.

exercises

1. What is an algorithm?
2. State in your own words the two required characteristics of an algorithm. Explain why each is necessary.

Look at the flowchart in Figure 1-1. On the basis of the flowchart, complete Exercises 3 through 8.

3. The first step in this algorithm is a decision-making step. State in your own words the decision that must be made.
4. What step is executed if a car is not available?
5. (a) What question on page 1 of the flowchart might be asked more than once?
   (b) If this question is asked more than once, what answer was given to the question the first time it was asked?
   (c) What answer would you expect to be given to this question the second time it was asked? (Notice that you might consider asking the question twice unnecessary, but the computer follows the steps of the algorithm exactly as they are presented.)
6. What happens if more than three persons are waiting for the barber?
7. What does the person who decides to wait his turn do while waiting?
8. (a) What is the maximum number of times that the question "Appearance satisfactory?" might be asked?
   (b) When will this occur?

Look at the flowchart in Figure 1-2. On the basis of the flowchart, complete Exercises 9 through 12.

9. Draw the symbol that marks both the beginning and the end of the flowchart.
10. Draw the symbol used for reading and writing.
11. What percentage is to be applied in computing commissions for sales in column B?
12. If an employee's sales in column A are $1430.00 and in column B are $820.00, what are the total wages for the current week?

Use both Figures 1-1 and 1-2 to do Exercises 13 and 14.

13. Draw the symbol that represents a step where a decision must be made.

14. How is sequence indicated on a flowchart?

15. Assume that you are responsible for supervising preparations for your local organization's garage sale. Develop algorithms for two of the tasks listed below.
    (a) Collecting items to be sold at the garage sale.
    (b) Handling advance and current-day publicity.
    (c) Securing facilities for the sale.
    (d) Organizing the work force for the sale.

PROCESSING DATA

Data processing is really only another name for paperwork. It is a series of planned actions and operations upon data to achieve a desired result. The methods and devices that achieve the result form a **data-processing system**. Regardless of the kind of data processed or the methods and devices used, all data-processing systems involve at least three basic elements:

- the source data, or **input**, entering the system
- the orderly, planned **processing** within the system
- the end result, or **output**, from the system

Let's consider a familiar situation to examine further what these terms mean. Assume a large dairy is preparing monthly statements for customers. The itemized record of a customer's purchases (the quantities of items purchased and their unit prices) is needed to compute the customer's bill. First, the quantities are multiplied by the unit prices. Applicable discounts are subtracted and taxes are added to this total to determine how much money the customer owes. Finally, the customer's monthly statement is printed and readied for mailing.

In this example, the *input* is the record of purchases with quantities and unit prices indicated. The *processing* includes the multiplication, addition, and subtraction required. The *output* is the customer's monthly statement of amount owed.

Now assume that a computer is used in this data-processing situation. One way to show the input, processing, and output involved is to draw a **system flowchart** as shown in Figure 2-1.

The leftmost symbol on the system flowchart is the **input/output (I/O) symbol** (☐). It always represents either input (data available for processing) or output (processed data—information—available for output). Since this symbol can be used for both input and output, it appears twice on this flowchart.

The rectangular symbol in Figure 2-1 is the **process symbol** (☐). It is a

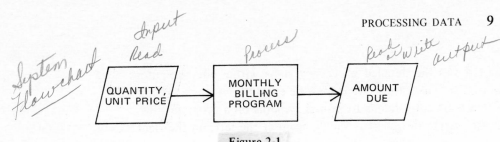

Figure 2-1

[handwritten annotations: System Flowchart; Input / Read; Process; Read or write / output]

general-purpose symbol indicating data transformation or data movement. When this symbol appears on a system flowchart for an electronic data-processing (EDP) system, it represents an action or series of actions performed by the central processing unit (CPU)—the carrying out of an algorithm expressed in a computer-program form.

One important function of a flowchart, discussed in Lesson 1, is to aid in problem analysis and solution planning. Another is to aid the problem solver in communicating ideas to others. To help standardize such communication, the **American National Standards Institute (ANSI)** has coordinated the development of a standard set of flowcharting symbols and associated meanings. We shall use many of these symbols in the flowcharts in this book. Their shapes and meanings are summarized in Appendixes A and B.

On a flowchart, brief explanations are given within the flowcharting symbols to further clarify what is being represented. While no standards govern what should be written within the symbols, some general guidelines apply. Unusual abbreviations should be kept to a minimum. If they are used, they must be defined. The amount of explanation within a symbol should also be kept to a minimum. It is often helpful to use the same variable names in both the flowchart and the computer-program form of the solution algorithm, provided that the variable names are indicative of their meanings.

Thus, a system flowchart shows the data, flow of work, and work stations within a data-processing system. We shall deal at first with simple problems requiring only one computer program for their solution, but a system flowchart may show the flow of work through several programs. (Two alternatives or supplements to system flowcharts are structure charts and HIPO diagrams. We discuss these design tools in Lessons 13 and 14.)

Although a system flowchart is very helpful in showing the inputs, major processing functions, and outputs of a data-processing system, it gives only a limited amount of detail about how the computer performs specific processing steps. The system flowchart in Figure 2-1 shows that a program for computing monthly bills is to be written and executed. It doesn't show which mathematical operations are needed, or the order in which operations must be performed. To provide this detailed information a second type of flowchart is constructed, called a **program flowchart**.

A program flowchart shows the detailed processing steps within one computer program and the sequence in which those steps must be executed. A single process symbol on a system flowchart corresponds to several symbols on a program flowchart. In Figure 2-2, the system flowchart is shown again at the left; on the right

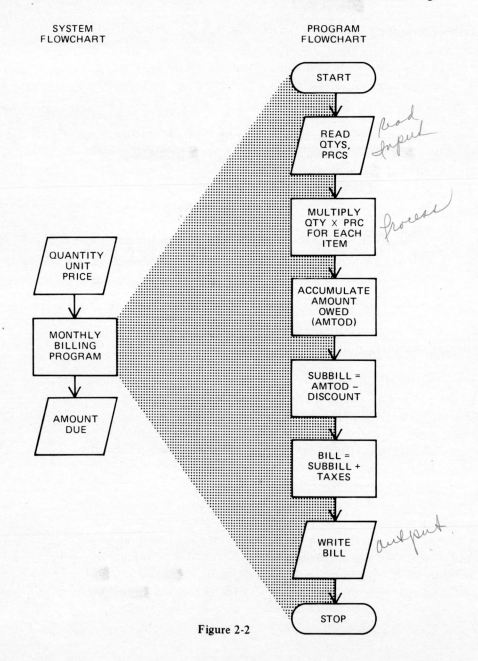

Figure 2-2

is a program flowchart showing the detailed processing steps of the monthly billing program. This program controls the sequence of operations required to prepare a monthly statement for one customer. (You may assume that the appropriate values for discount and taxes are obtained from a table that is set up as part of the program.) To produce the required output, the computer must perform **reading** and **writing** as well as arithmetic operations.

The input/output symbol and process symbol are basic symbols, used on both system and program flowcharts. Their general meanings are the same in both cases, but they show much more detail on program flowcharts. On a program flowchart, an input/output symbol shows the exact point during processing where data is accepted as input or provided as output. Similarly, on a program flowchart, a process symbol describes required processing specifically rather than comprehensively.

Other basic but very important symbols that appear on both system and program flowcharts are **flowlines.** As you have seen, these symbols indicate the sequence of required operations and the direction of data flow. The concept of **SIMPLE SE-QUENCE**, or the straightforward execution of one processing step after another, is basic to the design of a solution algorithm and to the computer-program representation of that algorithm. (We discuss this concept further in succeeding lessons.)

The normal direction of data flow on a flowchart is from top to bottom and from left to right. If the direction of flow of any flowline is not normal, an **arrowhead** must be used on the flowline. (If the direction of flow is normal, arrowheads are acceptable, but not required.)

Flowlines may cross. If they have no logical interrelation, no arrowheads should appear near their intersection. Two flowlines may join to form one line; in this case, a logical union or junction occurs in the flow, and one arrowhead is usually advisable.

Three flowlines may join another at a junction point. The resulting four flowlines are referred to as colinear in pairs. (The adjective *colinear* means in the same straight line.) One colinear pair must have opposing arrowheads near the junction point as shown below. A third arrowhead may be required for clarity.

Figure 2-2 shows a symbol used only on program flowcharts, the **terminal** or **interrupt symbol** (⬭). This symbol shows where a program begins, where its execution is delayed temporarily, or where it stops. Every program flowchart should begin with a terminal symbol containing START, located near the upper left corner of the first page of the flowchart. Since a terminal symbol is required at each point where a program may be interrupted, made to pause, or terminated, a number of terminal symbols containing END or STOP may appear on a program flowchart.

The distinction between system flowcharts and program flowcharts is important. As stated earlier, if a data-processing system comprises more than one program, the interrelationships of all the programs and data are shown on a single system flowchart. A program flowchart always deals with a single program. Lessons 3 through 10 of this book deal primarily with program flowcharts and with pseudocode as an additional tool of solution planning. In these lessons you will learn how to develop an algorithm for a well-structured program. Lessons 11 and 12 deal primarily with system flowcharts. Other design tools that facilitate a top-down approach to program development are described in Lessons 13 and 14.

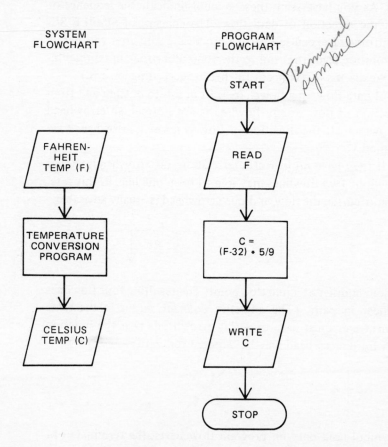

Figure 2-3

SAMPLE PROBLEM 2.1

Problem: The International Broadcasting Company wants a computer program that will accept a temperature reading expressed in Fahrenheit degrees as input, convert that value to Celsius degrees, and provide the result as output for its hourly weather report.

Solution: The system flowchart for this data-processing application is shown at the left in Figure 2-3. A program-flowchart representation of the solution algorithm, showing how the problem is to be solved, is given at the right. The terminal symbol containing START identifies the beginning of the program. First, the Fahrenheit value (F) is read as input. In the next step, a familiar mathematical formula is executed to convert this value from Fahrenheit to Celsius. Then the result (C, for Celsius) is written as output. Finally, program execution is terminated. This is a simple sequence of basic operations. When the program is executed by the computer, it will provide the solution to this problem.

exercises

1. (a) What is a data-processing system?
   (b) Name three basic elements involved in a data-processing system of any type.
2. (a) Identify the following symbols:

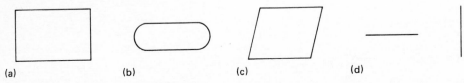

(a)   (b)   (c)   (d)

   (b) Which of the symbols should be used to show entry of data in the form of punched cards to an inventory-control program?
   (c) Which of the symbols should be used to represent the actual processing required in the inventory-control program?
3. Assume that the punched cards showing receipts and issues from inventory are one input to the inventory-control program. A magnetic-tape master inventory file indicating the inventory status before any of these additions or deletions occurred is another. The single output of the program is an updated master inventory file. Construct a system flowchart for this application.
4. Distinguish between system flowcharts and program flowcharts, showing how they are similar and how they differ.

5. (a) What is the normal direction of flow on both system and program flowcharts?
   (b) State a flowcharting guideline to be followed when the normal direction of flow is not adhered to on a flowchart.

6. The computer is to read values for regular hours, overtime hours, and hourly wage rate for one employee from a punched-card employee time card. Payment for regular hours is to be computed as rate times hours. Payment for overtime hours is to be computed at time and a half, or 1.5 rate times hours. The computer is to determine total pay for the employee for the week and print this total on a payroll register, from which checks will be printed later. Construct a program flowchart for this application.

7. What basic concept of computer-program design is exhibited on the flowchart that you drew in response to Exercise 6?

8. (a) How has the work of the American National Standards Institute (ANSI) affected flowcharting?
   (b) Why is this work important?

CHOOSING ALTERNATIVES

The programs discussed in Lesson 2 were very straightforward. The first one prepared a monthly statement for a dairy customer. The input values were quantities and unit prices; a simple sequence of processing steps was performed on the values; and a billing statement was written as output. The second program accepted a Fahrenheit value as input, performed a conversion, and provided a Celsius value as output.

It is often desirable to vary the sequence of processing steps within a solution algorithm to handle different kinds of input data or different situations that arise during processing. We want to take advantage of the logical decision-making capabilities of the computer.

Refer again to the task of preparing monthly statements to be mailed to the customers of a large dairy firm. Let us modify the problem slightly by stating that only customers whose bills exceed $200 (before taxes) are to receive a discount. A flowchart of an algorithm to solve this problem is shown in Figure 3-1. The diamond-shaped symbol is a **decision symbol** ($\diamondsuit$). It indicates that at a particular point in processing, a choice between two alternative paths, or sequences of instructions, is to be made.

Data is read into the computer. Quantities are multiplied by unit prices, and the amount owed by the customer is **accumulated** (collected together, to determine a final sum). Then a test is made: Is the amount owed (AMTOD) greater than ($>$) $200? Obviously, the question can be answered in either of two ways—yes or no. If the amount owed is not greater than $200, processing of the **main line** of the program continues. If the amount owed is greater than $200, a **branch**, or transfer of control, occurs. A decision point such as this is often called a **conditional branch**.

Notice that the test responses (yes and no) are clearly indicated on the flowlines from the decision symbol. This documentation is necessary, to make the flowchart easier to interpret, and programming errors less likely to occur.

Although we have shown one flowline extending down from the decision symbol and another extending from the right, that is not a requirement. For example, we might have drawn that portion of the flowchart as shown at the left in Figure 3-2.

A flowchart is one way of expressing the decision-making logic in this solution

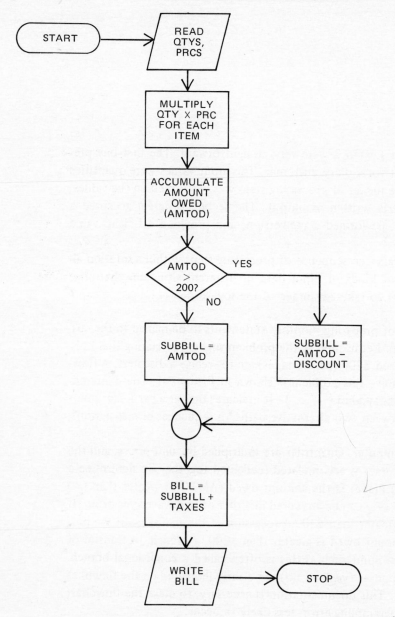

Figure 3-1

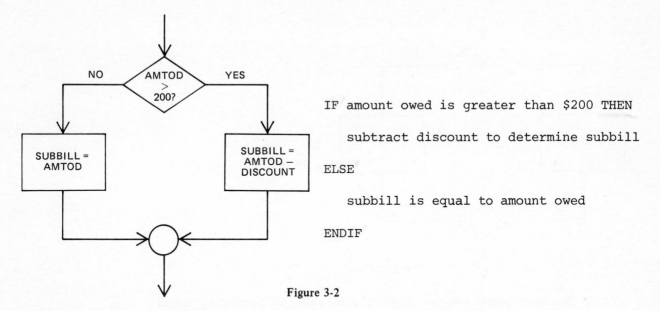

IF amount owed is greater than $200 THEN

   subtract discount to determine subbill

ELSE

   subbill is equal to amount owed

ENDIF

Figure 3-2

algorithm, but there are other ways as well. One technique that is rapidly gaining favor is the use of an informal language known as **pseudocode**. We can use pseudocode to express the same decision-making logic as shown at the right in Figure 3-2.

Just as flowcharts represent algorithms pictorially, pseudocode is a text form of representation. It is similar to some high-level programming languages (for example, FORTRAN and PL/I), but it does not impose the strict rules such as we must be willing to follow when actually writing a program. The pseudocode presents the solution algorithm in an easy-to-read, top-to-bottom fashion. For emphasis and clarity, the key words IF, THEN, ELSE, and ENDIF are written in uppercase letters. The THEN and ELSE clauses are indented three positions beyond the lines that precede them, while the key words ELSE and ENDIF are aligned with the IF to show that they are part of the same decision-making step.

Recall that in Lesson 2 we stated that the **SIMPLE SEQUENCE** pattern was basic to the design of an algorithm. Here we see another basic pattern, called **IFTHEN-ELSE**. Its general form is shown in Figure 3-3.

First, condition *p* is tested. *If p* is true, *then* statement *c* is executed and statement *d* is skipped. Otherwise (*else*), statement *d* is executed and *c* is skipped. Control then passes to the next processing step.

Before leaving this figure, it is important to note that a small, circular symbol called a **connector symbol** (○) is used in representing the decision-making logic within the IFTHENELSE pattern. It acts as a collector, emphasizing that the IFTHENELSE pattern has only one entry point and one exit point. When a connector symbol is used in this manner, it always has two flowlines entering and one

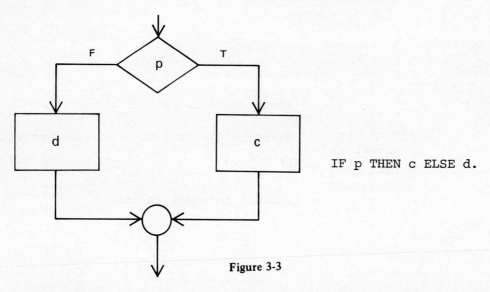

IF p THEN c ELSE d.

Figure 3-3

exiting. This means that it is *not* acceptable to allow either path extending from the decision symbol to go "off on its own," without returning to the point in the solution algorithm represented by the connector symbol. Any program in which such logic occurs is not a well-structured program.

Just for practice, let's look at another situation involving decision-making logic. Assume you are thinking about whether or not to attend a musical at a local auditorium. You might say: "*If* a ticket costs less than $6, *then* I shall go to the musical; otherwise (*else*), I shall stay home." Here you have identified a condition

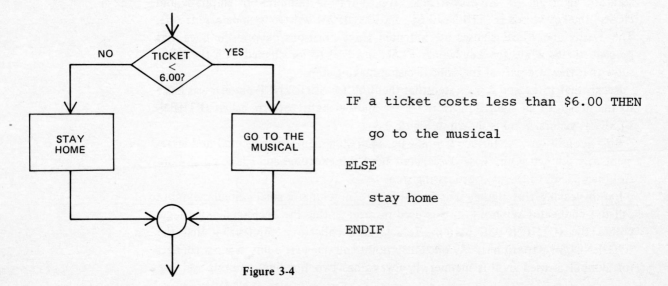

```
IF a ticket costs less than $6.00 THEN

    go to the musical

ELSE

    stay home

ENDIF
```

Figure 3-4

to be tested. You have also identified two alternative actions. Your decision-making logic follows an IFTHENELSE pattern. It can be expressed in flowchart or pseudo-code form as shown in Figure 3-4.

Now let's consider another problem statement:

An employee time card containing employee number, name, and hours worked is to be read as input. If the employee has worked more than 40 hours, his or her number, name, and hours worked are to be printed on a WEEKLY OVERTIME REPORT provided as output. If the employee has not worked more than 40 hours, no print action is required.

A program-flowchart representation of an algorithm to solve this problem is given at the left in Figure 3-5. The same algorithm is expressed in pseudocode form

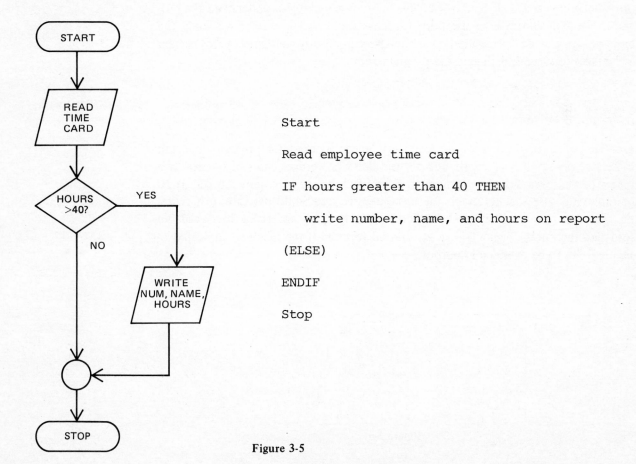

```
Start

Read employee time card

IF hours greater than 40 THEN

    write number, name, and hours on report

(ELSE)

ENDIF

Stop
```

Figure 3-5

at the right. This algorithm introduces one new idea: the "no-function condition," usually called a **null ELSE**. When the tested condition of the IFTHENELSE pattern (HOURS > 40, in this case) is true, we follow the true (yes) control path. When the tested condition is not true, no special alternative action is required. Thus, the false (no) control path goes directly to the connector symbol closing the IFTHENELSE. In pseudocode, the no-function condition is represented by enclosing the key word ELSE in parentheses.

As a systems designer or programmer, you may choose to use either program flowcharts or pseudocode, or both, in developing an algorithm. When confronted by a complex problem, it is often helpful at first to experiment with flowcharts until a method of solution is found. Then, the actual steps of the solution algorithm can be expressed in pseudocode form. An advantage of psuedocode is that it can be entered as comments in program coding or as part of the prologue for a program. Once there, it can be updated easily with computer help whenever the logic of the program is changed. It is readily available to anyone seeking to understand the program. We shall continue to use both flowcharts and pseudocode as we study the basic patterns of well-structured algorithms, because both techniques offer certain advantages to systems designers and programmers.

SAMPLE PROBLEM 3.1

Problem: The FunCola Bottling Company needs a computer program that can calculate the amount of credit due a customer who returns cases of bottles. If a case returned by a customer is more than half full, it is to be counted as full. If 10 or more full cases are returned, the customer receives $4.00 per case; otherwise, the customer receives $3.50 per case. The input to the program is a machine-readable card like the one in Figure 3-6. A preprinted form with the headings indicated in Figure 3-7 is to be provided as output.

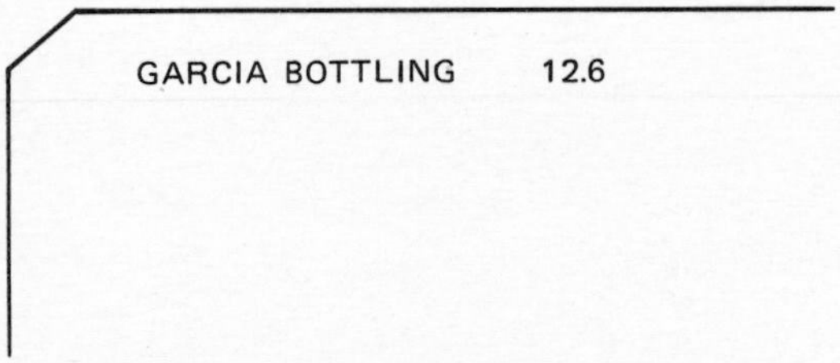

GARCIA BOTTLING   12.6

Figure 3-6

| FIRM | RETURN REPORT | | CREDIT AMOUNT |
	CASES RETURNED	FULL CASES CREDITED	

Figure 3-7

Solution: A solution to this problem is shown in both flowchart and pseudocode forms in Figure 3-8. We see here numerous examples of SIMPLE SEQUENCE and one IFTHENELSE.

The first step in finding the creditable number of cases returned is to read the number of cases actually returned (RETURN), as input. We add .5 to this input value. If the fractional portion of the input value is .5 or greater, this makes the integer portion of that value greater by one. This technique is known as "rounding up." Then we drop, or truncate, the fractional portion. Thus, only the integer portion is retained (in FULL), by what is effectively "rounding down." For example, if RETURN = 12.6, then RETURN + .5 = 13.1, and FULL (the creditable number of cases) = 13.

The program flowchart suggests that a built-in function INT such as is available in most programming languages be used to perform truncation. If such a function is not available, an alternative technique, such as shifting the result of the addition one position to the right to truncate the fraction, can be used.

FULL is then tested within the IFTHENELSE control structure to see if it is equal to or greater than 10. *If* it is, *then* the credit amount (AMT) is calculated as FULL times 4.00; otherwise (*else*), the credit amount is calculated as FULL times 3.50. Together with other values, the calculated credit amount is written on the preprinted form as output.

The pseudocode representation of this algorithm is straightforward and corresponds directly to the program flowchart. Note again the three-position indention used for the THEN and ELSE clauses of the IFTHENELSE pattern. Contrast this with the two-position indention used on the continuation line of the write state-

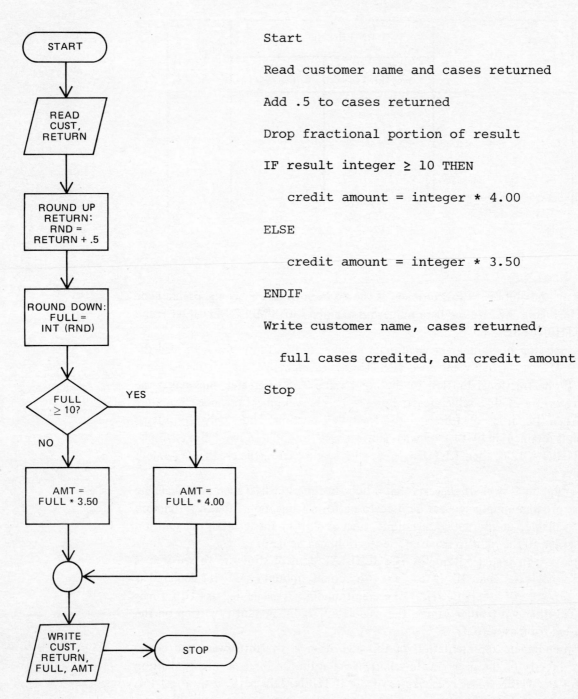

Start

Read customer name and cases returned

Add .5 to cases returned

Drop fractional portion of result

IF result integer ≥ 10 THEN

    credit amount = integer * 4.00

ELSE

    credit amount = integer * 3.50

ENDIF

Write customer name, cases returned,

   full cases credited, and credit amount

Stop

Figure 3-8

ment, which occurs simply because insufficient space is available on the first statement line. By following this method of indention consistently, the systems designer or programmer helps to make sure that others can understand readily the pseudocode representation.

exercises

1. State in your own words the purpose of a decision-making step in a solution algorithm. *It's easier to read*

2. What term is used synonymously with the term *decision-making step*? *IFthenElse*

3. Which of the following represents the question: "Is DUE greater than or equal to CREDIT?"

*I   A > B then
          S2
     Else*

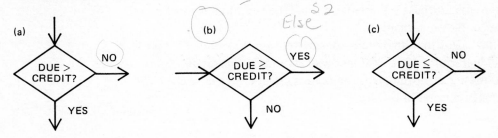

(a)   DUE > CREDIT?   NO   YES

(b)   DUE ≥ CREDIT?   YES   NO

(c)   DUE ≤ CREDIT?   NO   YES

4. (a) What is pseudocode? *Informal language*
   (b) What are some of the advantages that use of pseudocode offers? *easy to read*

5. (a) Using ANSI-approved flowcharting symbols, sketch the logic of an IF-THENELSE control structure. *connector symbol*
   (b) State the logic of the IFTHENELSE control structure in pseudocode form.
   (c) What pseudocode key words did you use in your response to Exercise 5(b)?
   (d) What indentions did you use in your response to Exercise 5(b)? Why?

6. (a) Explain what a null ELSE indicates.
   (b) Describe a problem in which a null ELSE occurs.
   (c) How is a null ELSE condition indicated on a program flowchart?
   (d) How is a null ELSE condition indicated when using pseudocode?

7. How is a connector symbol used in flowcharting an IFTHENELSE control structure? Why is it used?

Use Figure 3-8 to complete Exercises 8 through 12.

8. How is the number of cases returned by the customer determined?

9. On a price-per-case basis, is it to the customer's advantage to return more than 10 cases, or less than 10?

10. What amount is credited to a customer who returns 15.7 cases?
11. What amount is credited to a customer who returns 8.3 cases?
12. (a) Did you use the flowchart or pseudocode representation of the solution algorithm in responding to Exercises 10 and 11?
   (b) Why?

Assume the problem statement in Sample Problem 3.1 is modified in the following way: A customer is to receive no credit for returning a case that is only partially filled with bottles. However, the customer is entitled to $4.00 credit per case if eight or more full cases are returned. (Other parts of the problem statement remain unchanged.)

13. Redraw the program flowchart in Figure 3-8, modifying it to reflect the above changes in the problem statement.
14. Now modify the pseudocode representation of the solution algorithm in Figure 3-8 to reflect the same changes.
15. Using the solution algorithm that you constructed for Exercise 13 or 14, determine the amount credited to a customer who returns 56.7 cases of bottles.
16. On the basis of the same algorithm, what amount is credited to a customer who returns exactly nine full cases of bottles?

LOOPING

The solution algorithms discussed thus far have at least one characteristic in common: they show the program logic required to process only one set of input values. Generally, however, a computer program must be designed and coded to process many sets of input values. To provide for this, a program flowchart can be made to **loop**; that is, a sequence of processing steps can be done repetitively. An example is shown in Figure 4-1. Here six data values are read and added in an accumulator. After all six values have been added, their sum is printed as output.

This example is simple but informative. You can see that the YES flowline extending from the decision symbol is joined to another flowline at a right angle. This path is a branch back toward the beginning of the flowchart. In effect, a **program loop** is formed. A connector symbol serves as a collector at the beginning of the loop. As before, it has two flowlines entering and only one exiting. Its presence on the flowchart emphasizes that there is only one entrance point to the loop (at the connector symbol) and there is only one exit from it (at the decision symbol).

If (and only if) the tested condition is true (COUNT < 6), the processing steps along the true (YES) path are executed. If the tested condition is not true, the false (NO) path is followed. We say that the program loop is **exited.**

This loop pattern is another basic pattern of program logic. It is called **DOWHILE**. Note the key words DOWHILE and ENDDO in the pseudocode representation of the algorithm at the right in Figure 4-1. They are aligned at the left and mark the beginning and ending of the program loop, respectively. The processing steps within the loop are indented three positions for clarity.

The general form of the **DOWHILE** pattern is shown in Figure 4-2. To help you become familiar with this pattern, it is flowcharted in two ways. The same control structure appears in each representation; you should learn to recognize and use either one. First, condition q is tested. If q is true, statement e is executed and control returns to the test of q. If q is false, control passes to the next processing

[handwritten margin note: connector symbol serves as a collector at the beginning of the loop has 2 flow lines entering and 1 exiting]

[handwritten margin note: Dowhile & Enddo are pseudocode representation of algorithm.]

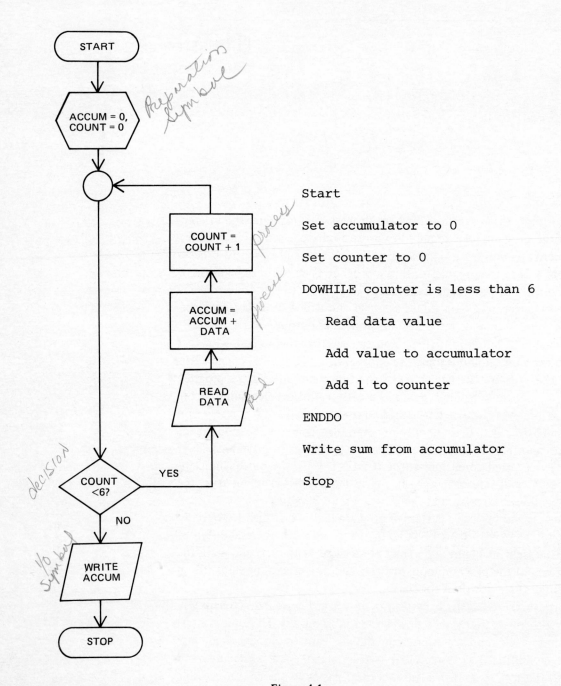

Start

Set accumulator to 0

Set counter to 0

DOWHILE counter is less than 6

    Read data value

    Add value to accumulator

    Add 1 to counter

ENDDO

Write sum from accumulator

Stop

Figure 4-1

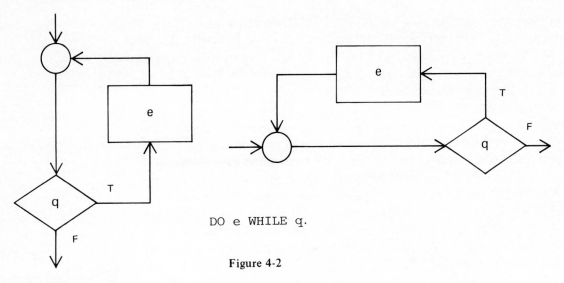

DO e WHILE q.

Figure 4-2

step. The DOWHILE pattern is always set up this way—the steps in the loop are executed while the outcome of the test is true. The loop is exited when the outcome is false.

Note that the DOWHILE pattern is a **leading-decision** program loop: the test of the condition occurs immediately upon entering the loop. Whether the additional steps inside the loop are executed depends on the outcome of the test. Remember, if the tested condition is not true, the loop is exited immediately following the test. Thus, if the tested condition is not true the first time it is tested, the remaining steps in the loop are not executed at all.

A new flowcharting symbol is introduced in Figure 4-1—the **preparation symbol** ( ). It represents an operation performed on data, or on a storage location reserved for data, in preparation for a major sequence of operations. Often this operation is performed before a program loop is first entered (as in this flowchart, for example); in these cases, it is referred to as an **initialization step.** In this algorithm, two storage locations are set to 0; one is used as an accumulator (ACCUM), and the other as a **counter** (COUNT). A counter is an example of a **loop-control variable**—a storage location whose contents are modified during the processing of a program loop, and tested elsewhere in the loop to determine whether or not the loop should be exited.

Though you may find it hard to realize at this time, it is important to note that any solution algorithm can be expressed using only the three basic patterns of logic we have learned thus far: SIMPLE SEQUENCE, IFTHENELSE, and DOWHILE. The theoretical framework for this approach—now known as **structured programming**—is usually traced to a paper by C. Bohm and G. Jacopini, initially published in Italian in 1965, then republished in English in 1966.[1] Their "structure theorem," which appears in that paper, is generally accepted as a proof of this claim. Also as early as 1965, Professor E. W. Dijkstra of the Netherlands insisted that programs using definite structuring were easier to write, read, and verify.[2] There is a fast-growing body of literature, documenting numerous program-development projects where this does indeed appear to be the case. Let us pursue this topic further.

When we construct an algorithm using only the three basic patterns of structured programming, we are at the same time taking advantage of another idea set forth by Bohm and Jacopini: the **building-block concept**. We have noted already that each basic pattern is characterized by a single point of entrance and a single point of exit. A SIMPLE SEQUENCE may be only a single statement, or it may be a series of single statements. It may also include IFTHENELSE patterns and DOWHILE patterns, and these may in turn include other SIMPLE SEQUENCEs comprising single statements, IFTHENELSEs, and DOWHILEs. We say that the contained patterns are **nested**.

A solution algorithm should have only one entry point and one exit point. For every basic pattern in the algorithm, there should exist a path from entry to exit which includes it. A computer program representation of such an algorithm can be viewed conceptually as a single statement. A program that can be viewed as a single statement is called a **proper program**.

A complete program can be set up using this building-block concept. In fact, we have already used this technique. Look at Figures 4-1 and 4-2. The general form of the DOWHILE in Figure 4-2 shows that if condition q is true, statement e is executed and control returns to the test of q. We used this general form in the algorithm in Figure 4-1, but instead of a single "statement e," several nested SIMPLE SEQUENCE patterns were executed whenever the tested condition was true.

Let's consider another problem statement:

> Machine-readable cards containing two items of data—a blood donor's identification number and blood type (A, AB, B, or O)—are provided as input. If a blood donor has blood type AB, his or her identification number is written as output on a report entitled "BLOOD TYPE AB REPORT." For cards showing

1. C. Bohm and G. Jacopini, "Flow Diagrams, Turing Machines and Languages with Only Two Formation Rules," *Communications of the ACM* 9, 5 (May 1966): 366–71.

2. Among Dijkstra's writings on this subject are: "GOTO Statement Considered Harmful," Letter to the Editor, *Communications of the ACM* 11, 3 (Mar 1968): 147–48; "The Structure of the THE Multiprogramming System," *Communications of the ACM* 11, 5 (May 1968): 341–46; and "Structured Programming," in J. N. Buxton and B. Randell, eds., *Software Engineering Techniques* (NATO Scientific Affairs Division, Brussels 39, Belgium), April 1970, pp. 84–88.

a blood type other than **AB**, no written output is required. The first input card contains a control value indicating the number of succeeding cards in the file. When all cards have been processed, program execution is terminated.

A program-flowchart representation of an algorithm to solve this problem is given in Figure 4-3. It contains a DOWHILE pattern that in turn contains a SIMPLE SEQUENCE consisting not only of single statements, but also of an IFTHENELSE.

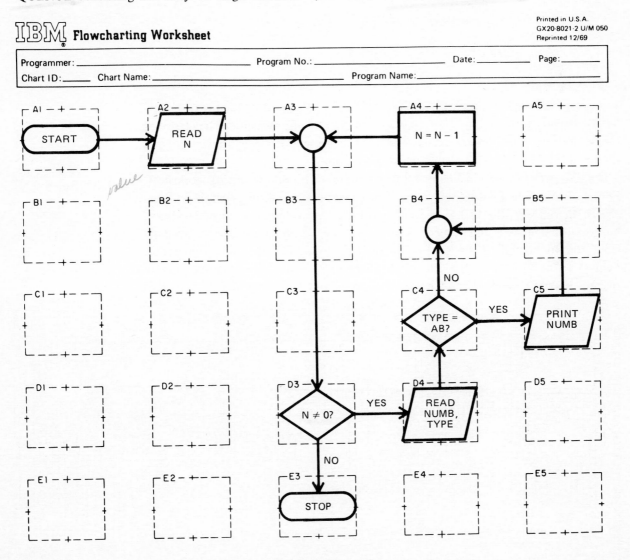

Figure 4-3

```
Start
Read control value
DOWHILE control value is not 0
    Read blood donor number and type
    IF type is AB THEN
        write number as output
    (ELSE)
    ENDIF
    Subtract 1 from control value
ENDDO
Stop
```

Figure 4-4

The same algorithm is shown in pseudocode form in Figure 4-4. In this form, the basic patterns and how they nest may seem more obvious. Because of its clarity of representation, many programmers tend to prefer pseudocode to flowcharting as their major tool in planning well-structured programs.

The program flowchart in Figure 4-3 is superimposed on a **flowcharting worksheet.** Forms of this type are designed to assist programmers in placing symbols on flow-charts. In full size, the 11 by 16½ inch worksheet provides an arrangement of 50 blocks with alphabetic and numeric coordinates: the ten horizontal rows are lettered from top to bottom—A to K; the five vertical rows are numbered from left to right—1 to 5. The blocks are aids for squaring up flowlines, maintaining uniform spacing between symbols, and providing coordinates (for example, A1 and K3)

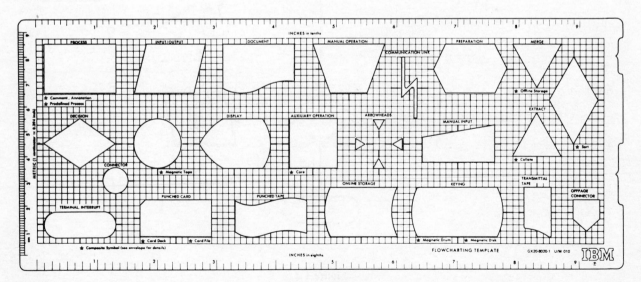

Figure 4-5

that can be referred to elsewhere on the flowchart. The worksheet itself is usually printed in light-blue ink so that its guidelines do not appear on photographic copies of the flowchart.

Another tool usually provided for the programmer's use is a **flowcharting template**. The template is a plastic or metallic card containing flowcharting symbols as cutout forms. The programmer can easily trace the outlines of the symbols needed for both system and program flowcharts. As an example, a flowcharting template made available by IBM is shown in Figure 4-5. The flowcharting symbols on this template generally comply with the American National Standards Institute (ANSI) and International Standards Organization (ISO) recommendations summarized in Appendixes A and B. Use of such templates not only is convenient, but also encourages uniformity in flowcharting, which in turn provides for better communication between the programmer and others who refer to the flowcharts.

SAMPLE PROBLEM 4.1

Problem: An instructor at Cloverdale School desires a computer program to compute and print a student's term grade. The individual scores earned by the student are to be entered as data on machine-readable cards and accumulated. Their sum is to be divided by the number of values added, to determine the student's term grade. Since the number of individual scores that must be added will depend on the number of assignments completed, a special card containing the student's name and the number of scores to be added must be provided as the first input to the program whenever it is used. The individual scores will follow as shown in Figure 4-6. The

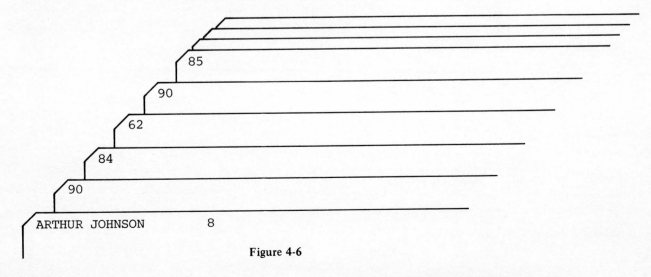

Figure 4-6

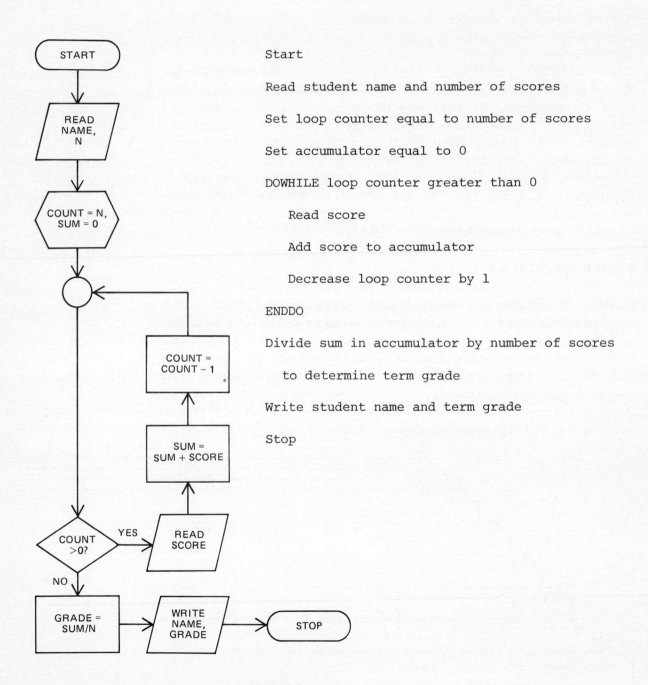

Start

Read student name and number of scores

Set loop counter equal to number of scores

Set accumulator equal to 0

DOWHILE loop counter greater than 0

    Read score

    Add score to accumulator

    Decrease loop counter by 1

ENDDO

Divide sum in accumulator by number of scores

   to determine term grade

Write student name and term grade

Stop

Figure 4-7

operating instructions for this job are to specify that multiple part paper is to be mounted on the printer, before the program is run; this will provide copies of the output for the instructor, the student, and the business office. Each copy of the output is to contain the student's name, the number of assignments completed, and the term grade computed by the program.

Solution: The algorithm in Figure 4-7 involves the use of a leading-decision loop, the DOWHILE pattern of structured programming. The loop will be executed N times, but we cannot simply decrease N by 1 each time through the loop. Why? Because we must have the value of N (that is, the number of scores added) to divide by, after we have summed all the scores. So we store the value of N in a loop counter (COUNT) as well, and we use the counter to control loop processing.

Note that by providing a value for N as input rather than "hard-coding" the number of scores as part of the solution algorithm (that is, coding a certain number in a program statement), we have provided the program flexibility called for in the problem statement. In a program intended for repetitive use, such flexibility is usually desirable.

A computer-program representation of this algorithm will be well-structured. It will use only SIMPLE SEQUENCE patterns and one DOWHILE pattern with nested SIMPLE SEQUENCE patterns. Since the program will have only one entry point and one exit point, it will be a proper program.

SAMPLE PROBLEM 4.2

Problem: The Car/Go Manufacturing Company produces a large number of automotive parts each year in its two plants. Some of these parts are returned to the main sales office because of defects in manufacture. A machine-readable card is prepared for each returned part, indicating part number, type of part, and date returned. Whether plant 1 or plant 2 made the part is determined manually by comparing the part number against previously generated computer reports of manufacturing output. A 1 or 2 is entered in position 1 of the card accordingly.

Car/Go needs a simple read-and-print program to process these cards and produce a printed listing of their contents for quality-control purposes. The number of defective parts which each plant manufactured is to be totaled for future reference. A special card containing 9 in column 1 will be positioned as the last card in the input deck as an end-of-file indicator (see Figure 4-8).

The output is to consist of a printed listing of the contents of the cards, followed by the two control totals.

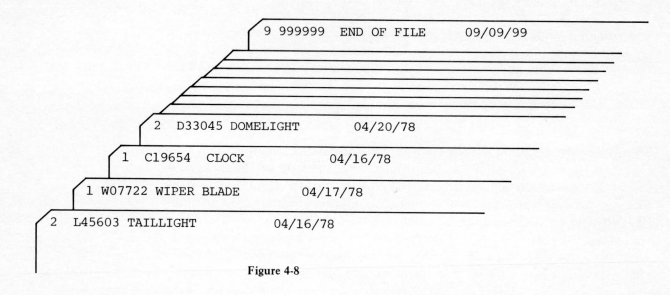

9 999999   END OF FILE   09/09/99

2   D33045 DOMELIGHT   04/20/78

1   C19654   CLOCK   04/16/78

1 W07722 WIPER BLADE   04/17/78

2 L45603 TAILLIGHT   04/16/78

Figure 4-8

Solution: A typical program, reduced to its most basic form, consists of input, processing, and output operations. As we noted earlier in this lesson, a program is usually designed to perform these operations on not just one, but many input values. Do you see these basic operations in the program flowchart of the solution algorithm in Figure 4-9? What other actions, not specifically called for in the problem statement, are specified in the program flowchart?

Note that the program prints a report heading. It is wise programming practice to identify all computer-generated printouts, whether or not the problem statement requires it. Doing so helps to insure that users of the output will know and understand what they receive.

As we noted before, storage locations used as counters or accumulators should be initialized before use. Here, two counters are set to 0. Note also that although there are only two valid card codes (1 and 2), the program logic must be such that it allows for human error in the preparation of input. Hence, a third possibility (anything other than 1, 2, or 9) is allowed for. It is essential to provide for the recognition and handling of bad input in any computer program that gets its data from an external source. The program does not have to process the bad data, but it should provide **feedback** to those responsible that an input error has occurred. In this case, the feedback is the message 'BAD INPUT' which precedes the printout of the card containing the invalid card code. For simplicity, error-handling steps have been omitted from some of the algorithms in this book. You should determine what error-handling procedures are needed, and you should be sure to include such steps in all of your programs.

If/M example

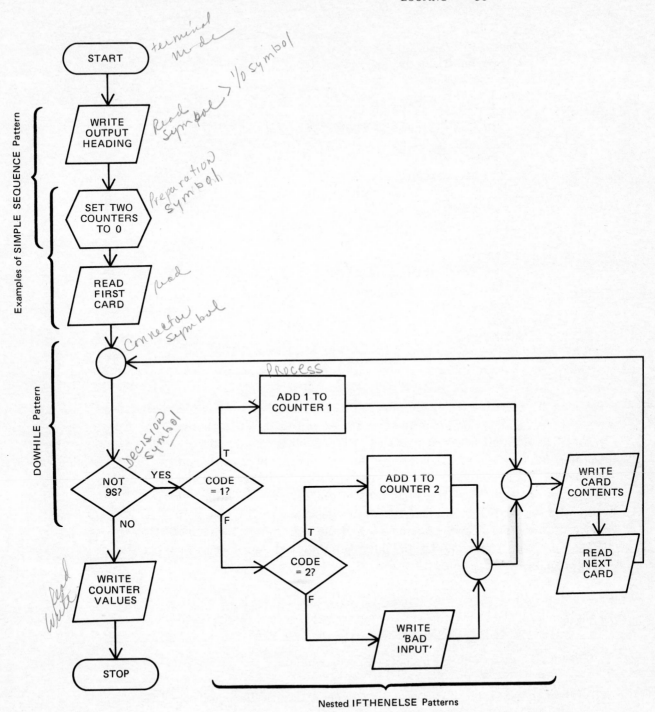

terminal mode

Read Symbol > I/O symbol

Preparation Symbol

Read

Connector Symbol

Decision Symbol

Read Write

PROCESS

Examples of SIMPLE SEQUENCE Pattern

DOWHILE Pattern

Nested IFTHENELSE Patterns

Figure 4-9

```
Start
Write heading on output
Set two counters to 0
Read first card
DOWHILE not 9s record
    IF code equals 1 THEN
        add 1 to counter 1
    ELSE
        IF code equals 2 THEN
            add 1 to counter 2
        ELSE
            write 'BAD INPUT' message
        ENDIF
    ENDIF
    Write contents of card
    Read next card
ENDDO
Write totals from counter 1, counter 2
Stop
```

pseudocode algorithm

Figure 4-10

The use of a special 9s record to indicate that all input data for a job has been processed is a common design technique. The 9s record serves as an end-of-file indicator. No attempt should be made to read additional records; special end-of-file processing—for example, the printing of final totals—should be carried out.

A DOWHILE pattern containing nested IFTHENELSE patterns and numerous examples of SIMPLE SEQUENCE are used in this solution algorithm. The DO-WHILE and nested IFTHENELSE patterns are indicated on the flowchart. They are evident in the pseudocode representation of the algorithm in Figure 4-10. The computer-program representation of this algorithm will be a well-structured, proper program.

exercises

1. State in your own words the purpose of a program loop.
2. What does it mean to say that a loop is "exited"?
3. (a) Using ANSI-approved flowcharting symbols, sketch the logic of a DO-WHILE control structure.
   (b) State the logic of a DOWHILE control structure in pseudocode form.

(c) What pseudocode key words did you use in your response to Exercise 3(b)?

(d) What indentions did you use in your response to Exercise 3(b). Why?

4. (a) Why do we call the DOWHILE pattern a leading-decision loop?

(b) What is particularly significant about the potential effects of this execution sequence?

5. Explain how the building-block concept can be used in developing a solution algorithm.

6. What is a proper program?

7. Name the three basic patterns of structured programming.

8. Explain two techniques for providing program flexibility based on the use of special values as indicators in the input job stream. (Hint: If you are in doubt, look again at Sample Problems 4.1 and 4.2.)

9. Construct a flowchart for a program to read individual records containing student names, addresses, and total number of accumulated credits as input. The names and addresses of all students who have earned 60 or more credits should be printed as output. For other student records, no action is required. Program execution should terminate when a special 9s record is encountered. Be sure to plan a well-structured program.

10. Repeat Exercise 9 above, but use pseudocode rather than flowcharting as a design tool.

11. Construct a program flowchart describing the processing steps needed to solve the following problem: Initial values of 5.00 and 3.00 are to be assigned to A and B respectively. A value for C, which is 95% of A, is to be computed. A, B, and C are to be printed. A is to be increased by twice the value of B. B is to be increased by 10%. The steps beginning with the computation of a value for C are to be repeated 5 times. Then program execution should terminate. Be sure to plan a well-structured program.

12. Assume the problem statement in Exercise 11 is modified as follows: A new value is to be computed for C on the first, third, and fifth passes through the loop only; otherwise, C is not to be changed. Express the solution algorithm for this revised problem statement in pseudocode form.

13. Look at your solution algorithm for the problem in Exercise 11 or 12.

(a) Are you computing any values unnecessarily on the last pass through the loop?

(b) If so, how might you modify the algorithm to avoid doing so?

(c) Suggest two or more reasons why retaining the algorithm that you have might be a preferable alternative to changing it.

14. Use either flowcharting or pseudocode to develop a solution algorithm for a program that will compute and print the sum of the numbers 1, 3, 5, 7, ..., 99. Be sure to plan a well-structured program.

ADVANCED DECISION MAKING

Often, a computer program must be designed and coded to handle a wide variety of inputs. We must provide flexibility in a solution algorithm, incorporating within the program an ability to process not only a variable *number* of inputs, but also whatever *type* of input is provided.

In business data-processing applications such as accounts receivable or employee payroll, large numbers of records are kept for reference purposes as relatively permanent data. Such data is not highly subject to change. Usually, it is needed for numerous business operations of the firm. Together, the data records constitute a **master file**. Current activities, or transactions, to be processed against the master file are called a **transaction file**, or **detail file**.

Assume, for example, that a firm's customer master records contain customer number, name, address, telephone number, and credit rating. Customer transaction records to be processed against this file might contain address changes, corrections to telephone numbers, and the like.

As another example, consider an inventory-control master file that contains stock status records of the numbers of various kinds of parts available for manufacturing planning. Each record contains several items, located in specific positions, or **fields**, of the record. These items indicate quantity in stock, quantity on order, quantity available for issue, and so on.

Transactions to be processed against this master file originate daily. They are assigned transaction numbers and punched into cards. A one-digit code is punched in column 1 of each card to indicate type of activity, as follows:

Code	Activity
1	Receipts (parts that arrive in response to previous orders)
2	Orders (requests for additional parts to be included in stock)
3	Withdrawals (also called issues; depletions from stock)
4	Adjustments (changes to stock levels for reasons other than those above, for example, transfers of parts to other manufacturing locations)

Our task is to design, code, and test a program to process the transaction records against the inventory-control master file. One page of a program flowchart we might construct in developing a solution algorithm is shown in Figure 5-1. This page summarizes activity identification and subsequent updating of the inventory-control master file.

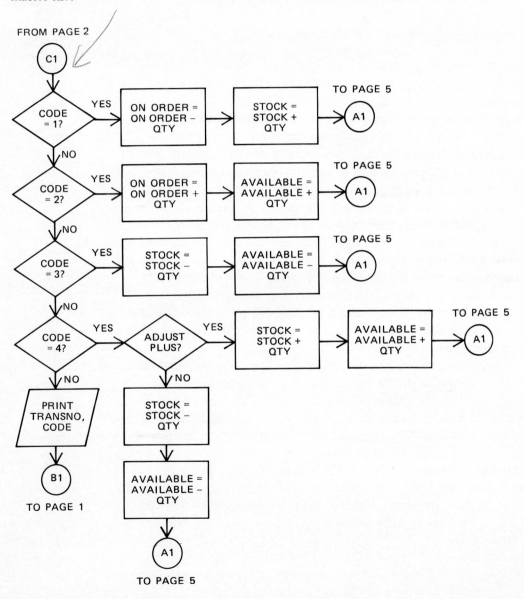

Figure 5-1

Assume that Figure 5-1 shows page 3 of the program flowchart. Note the connector symbols containing the label A1. When a flowline extends *to* a connector symbol, as all the flowlines extend to A1, the connector symbol shows *exit* to another part of the flowchart. Another connector symbol containing the same label, A1, but with a flowline extending *from* it to another symbol, must appear on some other part of the flowchart, indicating *entry* at that part of the flowchart. It shows the next processing step along any path having a corresponding exit connector symbol.

Now note the connector symbol containing the label C1 in Figure 5-1. Since a flowline extends from this symbol, we recognize that it is an entry symbol. The test for a code value of 1 is the next processing step along this path on the flowchart.

Connector symbols accompanied by page references (as are all in Figure 5-1) refer to corresponding symbols on other pages of a flowchart. Connector symbols containing labels but not accompanied by page references refer to corresponding connector symbols on the same page of the flowchart—this helps to avoid excessive intersecting of flowlines on a page. Remember that we have used connector symbols as collectors, to emphasize the beginning and ending points of the basic patterns of structured programming. Although no labels were shown inside the connector symbols, we could have included them if we wanted. There are no connector symbols used in this manner on the flowchart page in Figure 5-1.

Will a program coded according to the flowchart in Figure 5-1 be well-structured? It is not clear from the portion shown in the figure whether the basic patterns of structured programming, and only those patterns, are intended to be used. It certainly doesn't look like it. Before this question could be answered, more insight into the logic of this algorithm would be required.

Suppose that, instead of constructing a program flowchart, we set up the required decision-making logic in pseudocode form. The same series of tests for activity type are described using pseudocode in Figure 5-2. Here we see clearly a sequence of IFTHENELSE patterns. If a routine is executed, it processes the current transaction record. Then it returns control to this, the main line of the program, at the point where the transfer of control to the routine occurred.

This approach to the problem appears to yield structured logic. But it is not efficient. Assume we discover that a transaction is a receipt (that is, column 1 contains a code value of 1), for example. We execute the receipt routine, as indeed we should at this point. But, having done so, we go ahead and test the transaction repetitively thereafter, to see whether it carries code 2, 3, or 4 (or another unexpected value—the kind of situation that should never happen in programming, but will, and must be allowed for). Each of the succeeding tests yields a false outcome, but processing time is expended unnecessarily in making the tests.

Another point that should be noticed is the test determining whether or not the

```
IF code equals 1 THEN
    execute receipt routine
(ELSE)
ENDIF
IF code equals 2 THEN
    execute order routine
(ELSE)
ENDIF
IF code equals 3 THEN
    execute withdrawal routine
(ELSE)
ENDIF
IF code equals 4 THEN
    execute adjustment routine
ELSE
    execute exception routine
ENDIF
```

Figure 5-2

exception routine is executed: the truth or falseness of the condition "code equals 4." Since *all* transactions undergo this test, the exception routine will be executed for all but code 4 transactions. Therefore, it must contain logic to determine whether a transaction has already been processed successfully (that is, contains code 1, 2, or 3) or does in fact require exception processing.

Back to the drawing board! We need to improve our solution algorithm. Instead of using a consecutive sequence of independent IFTHENELSE patterns, let us use a **nested IFTHENELSE control structure**. This approach is flowcharted and shown in pseudocode form in Figure 5-3.

A new flowcharting symbol is introduced in Figure 5-3. It is the **predefined process symbol** (▯). This symbol is a means of referring to one or more operations (or routines) specified in detail elsewhere, such as in a reference manual or a different flowchart, but not in this flowchart. The printing inside the symbol summarizes the operations performed.

Now, if one of the tests for activity type yields a true outcome, the routine for that activity type is executed as before, but no additional tests for activity type are made. The entire nested IFTHENELSE control structure is exited, and program execution continues with the next processing step. The number of tests performed depends on the activity type. Only if all four tests are made and yield false outcomes does the exception routine get entered at all.

This nested IFTHENELSE control structure seems to meet our decision-making needs. Unfortunately, it is difficult to work with. What if we inadvertently omit a

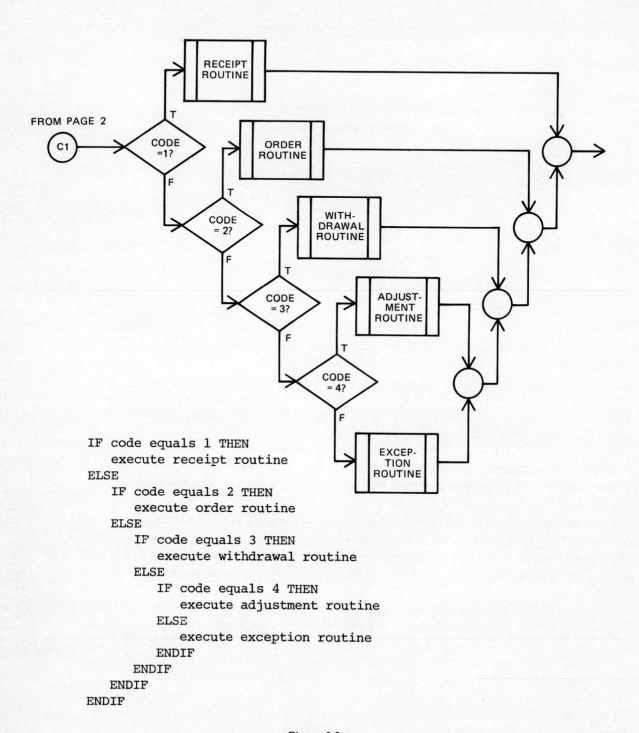

```
IF code equals 1 THEN
    execute receipt routine
ELSE
    IF code equals 2 THEN
        execute order routine
    ELSE
        IF code equals 3 THEN
            execute withdrawal routine
        ELSE
            IF code equals 4 THEN
                execute adjustment routine
            ELSE
                execute exception routine
            ENDIF
        ENDIF
    ENDIF
ENDIF
```

Figure 5-3

program statement corresponding to one of the closing ENDIFs? Or if we want to remove just one of the tests of activity type at a later time? Suppose we need to add a test for another activity type within the nested IFTHENELSE structure? The program coding to implement this structure must be done very carefully or errors will almost certainly occur. And what if there were 10, or even 100, possible activity types to be tested for? Obviously, many pages of flowcharting, or an unmanageable number of pseudocode indentions, would be required.

Fortunately, another option is available. We can replace the nested IFTHENELSE structure with a **CASE control structure**. CASE generalizes the IFTHENELSE basic pattern, extending it from a two-valued operation to a multiple-valued one. With one CASE control structure, we can represent all of the tests shown in Figure 5-3 (see Figure 5-4). Once we understand how this structure is derived, and see that it

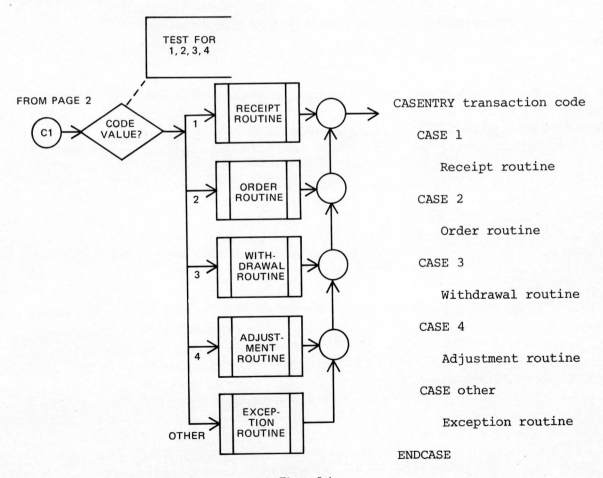

Figure 5-4

consists only of basic patterns, we can use it where we might otherwise resort to a nested IFTHENELSE.

The program logic in Figure 5-4 is the same as that shown in Figure 5-3, but it appears in a much more understandable form. By the simple use of parallel flow-lines, the same possible outcomes are documented. Generally, when this documentation technique is used, the first test to be made should be shown by the topmost flowline on the flowchart (or the leftmost one, if the parallel flowlines are vertical rather than horizontal). For processing efficiency, the test most likely to yield a true outcome should be made first, the next most likely one second, and so on; this helps to minimize the number of tests made on any one pass through this portion of the program.

The **annotation symbol** (---☐) is used on this flowchart to include explanatory material about the tests being documented. The use of this symbol is optional, but it permits us to insert additional information that will not fit inside the decision symbol. The annotation symbol can be used with other flowcharting symbols as well. It is connected to the symbol for the step it documents by a broken line, as shown in Figure 5-4.

We express the CASE control structure in pseudocode form using the key words CASENTRY, CASE, and ENDCASE as shown at the right in Figure 5-4. The text following the key word CASENTRY identifies the variable data on which tests are to be made. The text following each CASE key word tells the details of a particular test. For example, CASE 1 in Figure 5-4 represents a test to see whether the variable-data transaction code is equal to 1. The top-to-bottom arrangement of the CASE descriptions tells the order in which the tests are to be made.

As in other pseudocode representations of control structures, the three-position indentions shown in Figure 5-4 are not an absolute requirement. They help to emphasize the structure of the decision-making logic that is being described, however.

SAMPLE PROBLEM 5.1

Problem: In space laboratories, even computations involving only the basic arithmetic operations can be difficult, because the computations must be performed on extremely large or small numbers. Fortunately, the computer can be directed to handle such computations. This program is to accept three values as input (see Figure 5-5). The result of the computation is to be written as output.

Solution: A plan for the solution to this problem is expressed in pseudocode in Figure 5-6. The same algorithm is shown in flowchart form in Figure 5-7. The values provided as input to the program determine not only what result is written as out-

Operation Desired	Input		Notes
Division	D	dividend (A), divisor (B)	for A / B
Multiplication	M	multiplicand (A), multiplier (B)	for A * B
Subtraction	S	minuend (A), subtrahend (B)	for A - B
Addition	A	addend (A), augend (B)	for A + B

Figure 5-5

put, but also how the computer determines that result. The CASE control structure expresses the decision-making logic required.

Note that there are four valid operation codes, any one of which may be provided as the first input value for a run. But the program logic must allow for errors in input preparation, so a fifth control path (for "other" values) is provided. The feedback message 'BAD INPUT' precedes the normal printout of the result (0, in this error case), followed by the three input values.

It is good programming practice to **echo** (print a copy of) the input provided to a program run, as we have done here. A business report generated with computer help

```
Start
Read operation code, value for A, value for B
CASENTRY operation code
   CASE D
      Result = A / B
   CASE M
      Result = A * B
   CASE S
      Result = A - B
   CASE A
      Result = A + B
   CASE other
      Result = 0
      Write 'BAD INPUT' message
ENDCASE
Write result, A, B, operation code
Stop
```

Figure 5-6

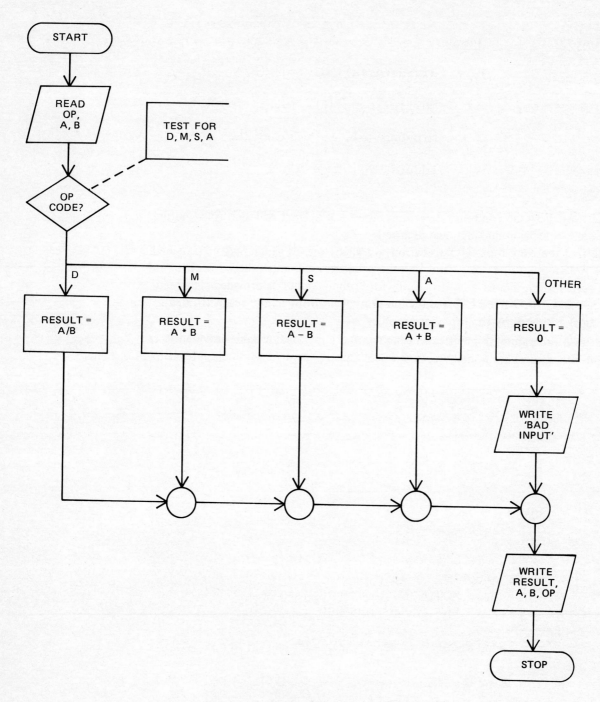

Figure 5-7

is much more meaningful if the input values used in generating the totals on the report as well as the totals themselves are displayed. The programmer who includes statements to display all inputs as well as all outputs, at least during the testing and debugging stages of program development, may save much programming time and effort. Doing so helps to insure that he or she really can determine what leads to what. The statements that cause display of the inputs can be removed from the final version of the program if necessary; for example, the volume of printing may lengthen the normal execution time of the program by an intolerable amount.

exercises

1. (a) Distinguish between master files and detail files.
   (b) Describe, in detail, some examples of each.

Use Figure 5-1 to complete Exercises 2 through 5.

2. How many of the tests shown will transaction records having activity code 1 undergo?
3. For what type of transactions will the most tests be performed?
4. What types of transactions cause the available stock quantity of a part to be reduced?
5. For what types of transactions is the next processing step shown at block A1 on page 5 of the flowchart?

6. Describe three types of flowcharting situations where use of connector symbols is necessary or advisable.
7. Explain how the decision-making logic represented by a SIMPLE SEQUENCE comprising IFTHENELSE patterns differs from that represented by a nested IFTHENELSE control structure.
8. (a) Using ANSI-approved flowcharting symbols, sketch the logic of a CASE control structure.
   (b) State the logic of the CASE control strucure in pseudocode form.
   (c) What pseudocode key words did you use in your response to Exercise 8(b)?
   (d) What indentions did you use in your response to Exercise 8(b). Why?
9. What does the order of the tests specified in Figures 5-6 and 5-7 imply?
10. (a) How are annotation symbols used in flowcharting? Why are they used?
    (b) Show by example a specific situation where use of an annotation symbol is advisable.
11. Construct a program flowchart containing a nested IFTHENELSE control structure to show the decision-making logic required in the following problem:

Sales commissions are computed for summer employees of a large department store as follows: 5% for all items in the range from $.00 through $50.00; 7% for all items in the range from $50.01 through $100.00; and 10% for all items in excess of $100.00. For each item that an employee sells during the day, a transaction record is created for subsequent batched input to an Employee Sales Commission program. The transaction record contains: the retail price of the item sold; a transaction code of 1, 2, or 3, indicating to which of the three commission categories the item belongs; and the employee number of the person who sold it. The Employee Sales Commission program computes the commission to be paid for each transaction record provided as input. It prints the retail price of the item sold, the commission, and the employee number of the employee who sold the item on a Daily Sales Commission Report. Execution of the program is terminated when a special transaction record containing 0000 as an employee number is processed.

12. Repeat Exercise 11 but use a CASE control structure rather than the nested IFTHENELSE to show the decision-making logic required. Express the algorithm in either flowchart or pseudocode form.

13. Look at the algorithm that you constructed for Exercise 12. Does it provide for the processing of invalid input, that is, transaction records not containing 1, 2, or 3 as transaction codes? (In this respect, the problem statement in Exercise 11 is incomplete.) If not, modify the algorithm to print the message INPUT ERROR and the current values of retail price and employee number on an exception report whenever invalid input is encountered.

14. Modify the algorithm that you constructed for Exercise 12 to incorporate the following additional function: For all sales for which a commission in excess of $25.00 is computed, the employee number of the person making the sale, the retail price of the item sold, and the commission are to be printed on a special exception report intended for management.

MORE ABOUT PROGRAM LOOPS

By now you have acquired some familiarity with the three basic patterns of structured programming: SIMPLE SEQUENCE, IFTHENELSE, and DOWHILE. You can express these patterns in either flowchart or pseudocode form.

In Lesson 5, we saw how a series of tests may be set up as a nested IFTHENELSE control structure. We learned a shorthand notation to substitute in its place: the CASE control structure. The CASE structure describes the same kind of decision-making logic as a nested IFTHENELSE, but more conveniently. Since the CASE structure consists entirely of basic structured programming patterns, we can use it with confidence that we are maintaining structure in our solution algorithm. The computer-program representation of the algorithm will be a well-structured program.

Another common combination of the basic patterns of structured programming is a SIMPLE SEQUENCE and a DOWHILE. This combination is shown in its general form in Figure 6-1(a). First, statement e is executed. Then we test for the condition *not q* (indicated by q with a line over it, or $\bar{q}$). We continue to *do* statement e *while* condition $\bar{q}$ is true. Note that when condition $\bar{q}$ is false, we have *not $\bar{q}$*—therefore q! If you find this negative logic confusing, don't be discouraged. So do lots of other systems designers and programmers.

It's precisely for this reason that the **DOUNTIL control structure** has come into common use. This structure is shown in Figure 6-1(b). We can summarize the program logic as follows: *do* statement e *until* the condition q is true.

To be sure we understand this logic, let's consider how it might apply to an ordinary situation. Suppose, for example, that you are employed as a sandwich-maker in a neighborhood delicatessen. Your employer may say: "Make one beef sandwich. Continue to make (*do*) beef sandwiches *while* you *are not* too tired to do so." This is the pattern of logic shown in Figure 6-1(a). Alternatively, your employer may

(a) SIMPLE SEQUENCE and DOWHILE

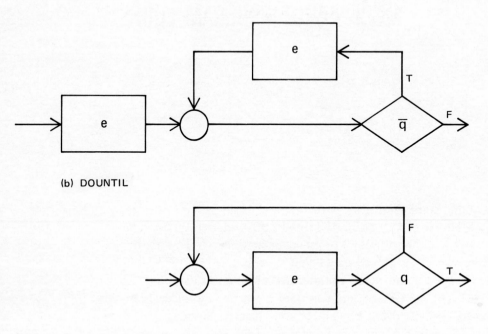

(b) DOUNTIL

Figure 6-1

say: "*After* you have made one beef sandwich, continue to make (*do*) beef sand-wiches *until* you *are* too tired to do so." This is the pattern of logic shown in Figure 6-1(b).

What is the significant difference between the **DOWHILE** pattern that we have learned to use and this combination of **SIMPLE SEQUENCE** and **DOWHILE** known as **DOUNTIL**? We saw earlier that the DOWHILE pattern is a leading-decision program loop: the test for the loop terminating condition is made immediately upon entering the loop. In contrast, the DOUNTIL pattern is a **trailing-decision** program loop: the test for the loop terminating condition is not made until the other processing steps in the loop have been executed. This means that no matter what the outcome of the test within the loop, the processing steps that precede the test will always be performed at least once, before the test is made. So before using DOUNTIL we must be sure that we *want* to perform the functions within the loop at least once. How many more times we perform the functions within a trailing-decision loop depends on the outcomes of any successive tests. The execution of the processing steps in the loop and subsequent condition testing continue until the tested condition is known to be true. Then the loop is exited.

Note that a DOWHILE control structure is exited when the tested condition is false, but a DOUNTIL is exited when the tested condition is true. It is essential to set up all loop constructs in a solution algorithm in this manner. Otherwise, the computer-program representation of the algorithm will not be a well-structured program.

In Lesson 4, we discussed numerous DOWHILE loops that were executed once, re-executed, or exited on the basis of the current value of a loop counter. (See the tests for COUNT < 6 in Figure 4-1, N $\neq 0$ in Figure 4-3, and COUNT > 0 in Figure 4-7.) The execution of a DOUNTIL loop can be controlled in a similar manner. We initialize the loop counter to its starting value before entering the loop. With each execution of the loop, we increase (or decrease) the value of the counter and then test its value to determine whether or not the processing steps within the loop should be re-executed.

The flowchart in Figure 6-2 shows how to read six data values, add them together in an accumulator, and write their sum, using a DOUNTIL program loop. We achieved exactly the same result using a DOWHILE program loop in Figure 4-1. Compare the tests for loop termination in these algorithms. As we have said, the DOWHILE program loop is exited when the tested condition is false; the DOUNTIL program loop is exited when the tested condition is true.

Consider the following problem statement:

A table is to be generated with computer help, showing the storage costs for personal property at a large warehouse. The table covers property values from $1000 through $20,000, in increments of $100. Storage costs are computed at 5% of property values. Each table entry is to consist of a property value and a corresponding storage cost. Some examples are:

$$
\begin{array}{ll}
\$1000 & \$50 \\
1100 & 55 \\
1200 & 60 \\
\cdot & \cdot \\
\cdot & \cdot \\
\cdot & \cdot
\end{array}
$$

A program flowchart of an algorithm to solve this problem is given at the left in Figure 6-3. It contains a DOUNTIL pattern and numerous examples of SIMPLE SEQUENCE. The same algorithm is shown in pseudocode form at the right.

Here, the loop control variable is not a specially introduced data item. Instead, it is one of the data items discussed in the problem statement: the personal property value (PROP). We initialize PROP to its starting value, $1000, before we enter the DOUNTIL loop. Upon entering the loop, we use this value immediately in comput-

DOUNTIL program loop
Exit when tested condition
are true.

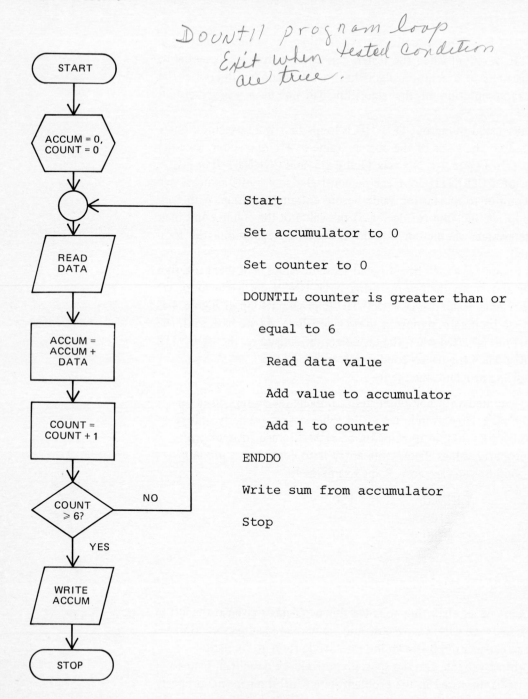

```
Start

Set accumulator to 0

Set counter to 0

DOUNTIL counter is greater than or

    equal to 6

      Read data value

      Add value to accumulator

      Add 1 to counter

ENDDO

Write sum from accumulator

Stop
```

Figure 6-2

Dountil pattern with numerous
example of Simple Sequence

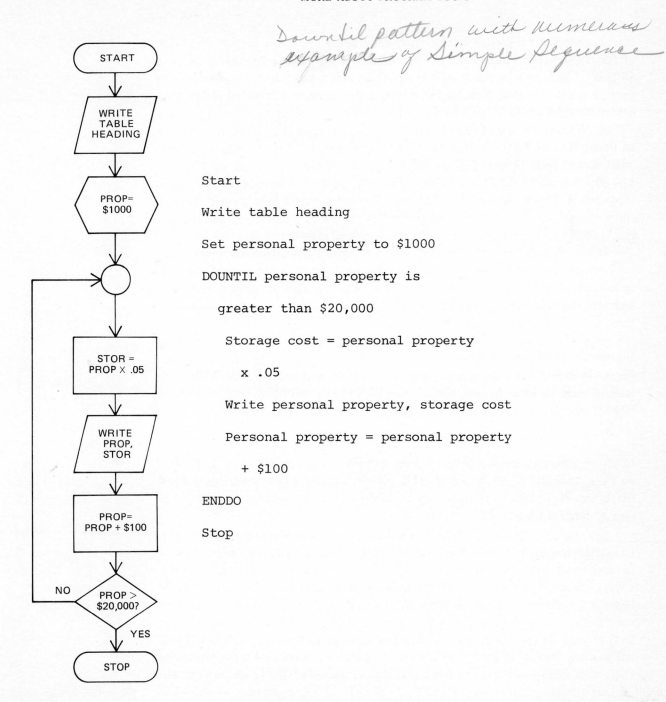

```
Start

Write table heading

Set personal property to $1000

DOUNTIL personal property is

   greater than $20,000

     Storage cost = personal property

       x .05

     Write personal property, storage cost

     Personal property = personal property

       + $100

ENDDO

Stop
```

Figure 6-3

ing a storage cost, and print a table entry accordingly. Next, we increase the value of PROP by $100. Finally, we test the value of PROP to see whether it exceeds $20,000. The loop is re-executed if the tested condition is false; it is exited if the tested condition is true. Note that one table entry has been computed and printed before the value of the loop control variable is tested.

How do we know to set PROP to $1000 initially, increase it by $100, and test for an upper limit of $20,000? Because of the requirements of the problem statement. What would have happened if we had tested for PROP = $20,000, or PROP $\geq$ $20,000, instead of PROP $>$ $20,000? The loop would not have been re-executed when PROP had a value of $20,000. No table entry would have been created to show the storage cost for personal properties valued at $20,000, so the requirements of the problem statement would not have been satisfied.

A DO statement designed especially for loop control is available in several common programming languages. The programmer who uses such a statement need not code separate statements to initialize, increase (or, in some languages, decrease), and test the value of a loop control variable. The single DO statement causes all three to be done automatically.

To use a DO statement correctly, the programmer must know the order in which the initialize, modify, and test operations controlled by the DO statement will occur. In most PL/I implementations, the DO statement sets up a DOWHILE, or leading-decision, loop. In fact, there is one PL/I DO statement where both DO and WHILE are used as keywords. For example, the PL/I programmer may write

DO WHILE (TIME $<$ = INHOUR);

to set up a leading-decision program loop, exactly as we have described it. There is no PL/I capability to set up a DOUNTIL pattern directly, so the programmer must use other PL/I statements to set up DOUNTIL logic. We discuss this matter in greater detail in Chapter 8.

A DO statement is also available in the FORTRAN programming language. This DO statement sets up a DOUNTIL, or trailing-decision, loop. This means that, once the DO statement is encountered in a FORTRAN program, the loop it introduces is always executed at least once. If the problem situation is such that there may be times when the loop should not be executed at all, the FORTRAN programmer must insure that the code at this point "does nothing" gracefully. One way of doing so is to precede the DO statement by an IF statement—a separate, explicit test that will cause a transfer of control before the DO statement is reached if the processing steps within the loop should be bypassed. The complete DOUNTIL loop can be one of the two alternative control paths of an IFTHENELSE pattern, as shown in Figure 6-4.

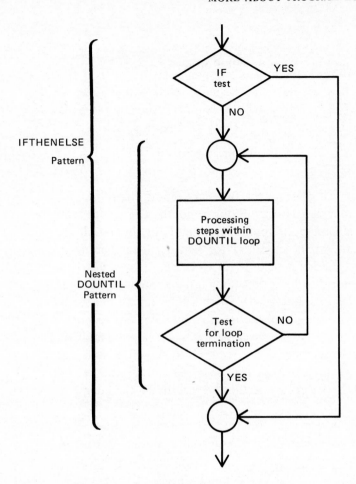

Figure 6-4

Even for DOUNTIL loop processing, the capabilities of the FORTRAN DO statement are very limited. The only condition that can be tested for is whether a particular variable used as a loop counter has a particular value. The only operation that can be performed on the variable is to increase its value by a fixed amount each time the loop is executed. In common practice, we often want to test for any of a great variety of other possible conditions. We may want to decrease a counter rather than increase it. Often, as in the storage cost table algorithm above, we do not want to control loop processing by a counter at all. For these reasons, FORTRAN programmers tend to use statements other than DO to set up both DOWHILE and DOUNTIL patterns. (As noted for PL/I, we discuss setting up structured-programming logic in FORTRAN in greater detail in Chapter 8. Writing structured programs in COBOL and BASIC is also discussed in that chapter.)

SAMPLE PROBLEM 6.1

Problem: Harris Wholesale Distributors maintains comprehensive records of the type, volume, and sales price of all merchandise dispatched from its warehouse locations. These records are updated daily with computer help, and provide the basis for numerous management inquiries as well as for weekly sales reports. As a part of year-end processing, a summary report showing monthly sales volume—the total dollar value of all merchandise dispatched from the warehouses each month—is needed.

The input to the program that will generate the summary report comprises one record for each warehouse that reported activity during a month. The record tells the name and location of the warehouse, its total sales volume for the month (in dollars), and a numerical indicator of the month: 1 for January, 2 for February, and so on (see Figure 6-5). Since the input records are to be read from a distribution master file, they can be assumed to be in ascending order by month (all January records first, then February records, and so on). There will be at least one warehouse record for each month. A special end-of-file record containing two asterisks in the month-indicator field, zeroes in the sales-volume field, and no data in other fields will be provided as the last input record. This record is to be written as a separator line preceding the year-end total line on the report. More importantly, its presence on the report will serve as a verification that all records on the input file have been processed.

The summary report is to contain one print line for each warehouse record, that is, for each warehouse from which merchandise was dispatched during a particular

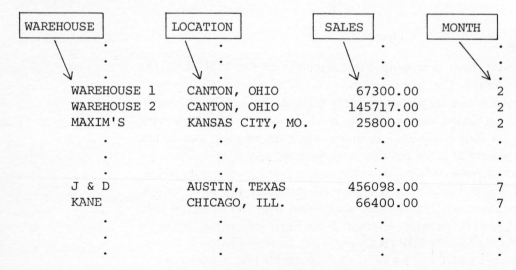

Figure 6-5

```
                    HARRIS WHOLESALE DISTRIBUTORS

                    YEAR-END TOTAL SALES REPORT


MONTH   WAREHOUSE                LOCATION                      SALES

Jan.    Tompkin's                Aberdeen, Maryland        45,069.00

        Warehouse A              Des Moines, Iowa          44,036.00
                                                                 .
                                                                 .
                   JANUARY TOTAL SALES VOLUME         $3,846,077.00 *
                                                                 .
                                                                 .
**                                                             .00
                   YEAR-END TOTAL SALES VOLUME      $51,994,223.00 **
```

Figure 6-6

month. When all records for a month have been read and printed, a total sales volume for the month is to be printed. A grand total indicating the sales volume for the year is to be printed at the end of the report. (See Figure 6-6.)

Solution: The program logic required in this solution algorithm is best satisfied by a DOUNTIL control structure. (See Figures 6-7 and 6-8.) One complete execution of the program loop is needed for each month. Since we know that there will be at least one warehouse record for each month, we know that the processing steps within the loop must be executed at least once (indeed, at least twelve times). How many more times some of the steps in the loop are executed depends on how many more records there are for the months.

An **IFTHENELSE** pattern within the **DOUNTIL** control structure causes a monthly total line to be printed whenever the first warehouse record for a new (succeeding) month is read. In other words, each complete execution of the program loop causes the summary statistics for all warehouses for a particular month to be listed, and the total sales for the month to be printed. Then the storage location used for the monthly total (**MONSUM**) is re-initialized to 0. The monthly index (**I**) used to keep track of the current month is increased by 1 so it matches

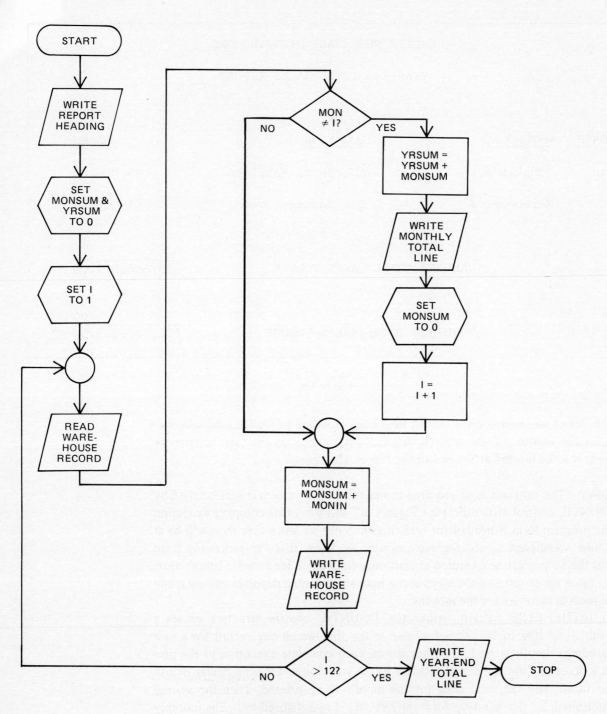

Figure 6-7

```
Start
Write report heading
Set accumulators for monthly and year-end
   totals to 0
Set monthly index to 1
DOUNTIL monthly index is greater than 12
     Read warehouse record
     IF input month is not equal to monthly index THEN
         add monthly total to year-end accumulator
         write monthly total line
         set accumulator for monthly total to 0
         increase monthly index by 1
     (ELSE)
     ENDIF
     Add sales volume to monthly accumulator
     Write warehouse record
ENDDO
Write year-end total line
Stop
```

Figure 6-8

the month-indicator field (MON) of the first warehouse record read for a succeeding month.

There will be 12 complete executions for the 12 months' data, plus a final execution for the special end-of-file record. In this final execution of the loop, the two
asterisks in the month-indicator field (MON) will be compared to the current value
of the monthly index (I); at this point, I equals 12. The compared values will not be
equal. This will cause the monthly total for December to be added to the yearly
total, the monthly total line for December to be printed, and I to be increased by
one. The line containing two asterisks will then be printed. The DOUNTIL loop will
be exited, because the current value of I (13) is greater than 12. The year-end total
line will be printed, and program execution will be terminated.

exercises

1. (a) What kind of a program loop is formed in a **DOWHILE** pattern? *leading decision program loop*
   (b) What kind of a program loop is formed in a **DOUNTIL**? *trailing decision program loop*
   (c) When is the difference between **DOWHILE** and **DOUNTIL** particularly
       important? Why?
2. Modify the program flowchart shown in Figure 6-2 to make a more general-

purpose solution algorithm. The revised algorithm should describe how to read and add any number of data values (not just 6). A count of the number of values added should be printed along with the sum of the values.

3. Now modify the pseudocode representation in Figure 6-2 to reflect the same logic as the flowchart you constructed in response to Exercise 2.

4. (a) If condition q is "X is less than or equal to Y," what is condition $\bar{q}$?
   (b) If condition $\bar{q}$ is "A + B < C," what is condition q?

5. Assume that the problem statement for Sample Problem 6.1 is modified by deleting the statement "There will be at least one warehouse record for each month." Change the program flowchart shown in Figure 6-7 accordingly.

6. Repeat Exercise 5, but change the pseudocode representation of the algorithm.

7. Construct a program flowchart describing the processing steps needed to solve the following problem: One data item, MULT, is to be read as input. The sum of the following operations is to be computed and printed: 1, 1 + 1*MULT, 1 + 2*MULT, . . ., 1 + 9*MULT. Be sure to plan a well-structured program.

8. Repeat Exercise 7, but use pseudocode rather than a program flowchart to plan the processing required.

9. Construct a program flowchart or use pseudocode to plan the processing steps needed to find the area and perimeter of a rectangle. The input will be the length and width of the rectangle, expressed in inches. Display the input values as part of the output. Be sure to identify all of the values printed, so that the output can be readily understood.

10. Repeat Exercise 9, but now find the area and circumference of a circle rather than the area and perimeter of a rectangle. Assume that one value, the diameter of the circle, expressed in inches, is provided as input.

USES OF DESIGN DOCUMENTS

We've discussed the importance of both system and program flowcharts as instruments of communication in previous lessons. A system flowchart identifies data and directions of data flow in a problem situation. It shows the major steps, or work stations, through which data must pass. A program flowchart identifies the detailed processing steps within one major step on a system flowchart. As communication tools, flowcharts can exist at various levels of detail. Some are very simple, such as a symbol containing "do the payroll"; some are very detailed, showing each processing step. Each level of flowcharting serves a different audience. Manager of departments using computer-generated output, individual users, internal and external auditors, data-processing management, operations personnel, systems analysts, and other systems designers and/or programmers may need to refer to flowcharts. At the very least, the flowchart is a means of communication from a systems designer or programmer to himself or herself, at a later time.

A flowchart also serves as a vital analytical tool. For example, a business applications or scientific programmer uses the flowchart as a means of testing various approaches to a problem—laying out the problem-solving logic. The programmer starts with symbols that represent the major functions of a candidate solution algorithm. Next, flowlines are drawn to connect the symbols, thereby showing the interrelationship of input/output functions, steps for performing computations, and decision-making functions. By testing various approaches, the programmer can eliminate any that do not solve the problem and can select from those that do, the most satisfactory algorithm for the particular problem. This task involves trial and error. No one draws a complex, complete flowchart requiring no modifications, in the very first attempt.

Pseudocode is rapidly gaining favor as a program design tool. Its primary advantage is that it permits the programmer to express evolving ideas about the required program logic in a very natural, easily understood form. The programmer is free to concentrate on the solution algorithm, rather than on the form and constraints within which it must be stated. The result is an unambiguous representation of the solution to the problem.

When the programmer is satisfied that all processing steps, alternatives, and exceptions have been identified and provided for, the solution algorithm (in whatever form the programmer has expressed it) should be verified. The objective is to prevent errors from occurring, or, if some have already occurred, to detect and eliminate them as soon as possible. In the past the major portion of a programmer's time has not been spent in program design and coding, but rather in debugging and testing. Now many computer professionals are insisting that this need not be the case: *a program can be written correctly, so that it executes properly the very first time it is run.* A careful, early verification of the program design, or solution algorithm, is an essential step in achieving this objective.

Under one approach to verification of design, the design documentation is distributed to selected reviewers, who are asked to study it and respond within an established time period. Every reviewer is directed to note, individually, any changes, additions, and deletions required. This approach is known as an **informal design review**.

Another approach that is gaining favor is the use of **structured walk-throughs**. At this point in algorithm development, the walkthrough is a **formal design review**. Here, the design documentation is made available to from two to four people selected to serve as members of a review team. After they have had time to prepare, these reviewers meet together with the program designer and a moderator for an established time period, usually about two hours. Each reviewer is expected to have studied the design documentation and is asked to comment on its completeness, accuracy, and general quality. Then the moderator "walks" the group through each step of the documentation, covering any points raised by the review team.

How does one start when reviewing a solution algorithm set forth in a program flowchart, pseudocode, or other form of design documentation? Some reviewers, individually or in groups, find that pretending to be the computer works well. Representative values for all types of input are selected: (1) data that is normally expected, (2) valid but slightly abnormal data (for example, minimum and maximum values allowable), and (3) invalid data. The individual or group follows the problem-solving logic step by step to process the input and determine what output will be produced. If the output matches predetermined correct results, the logic within the solution algorithm is upheld. Pretending to be the computer in this way is called **simulation**, **procedure execution**, or **desk checking**. While tracing the problem-solving logic, each reviewer must be careful not to make any assumptions. The computer can only do what it is told; it is unable to make assumptions.

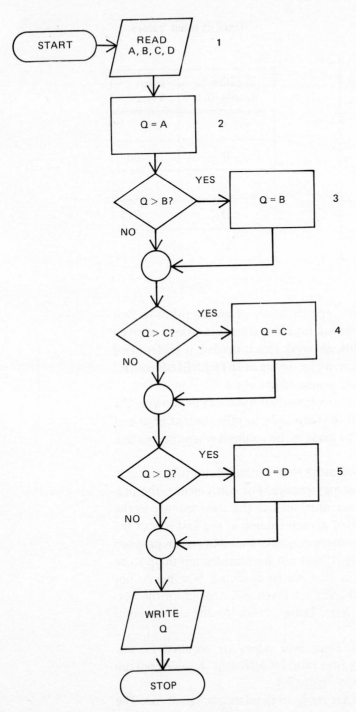

Figure 7-1

Table of Storage Locations

Table of Input Values

	A	B	C	D	Q
START	k	k	k	k	k
1					
2					
3					
4					
5					

Figure 7-2

Location to Receive Data	Input Value
A	493
B	.06
C	5
D	.015

Figure 7-3

Figure 7-1 shows the program-flowchart representation of an algorithm to find the smallest of four numbers. The numbers are read into storage locations reserved for the variables A, B, C, and D. One additional work area is needed; it is identified by the variable name Q. Comparisons are made by means of IFTHENELSE control structures. The smallest of the four numbers is printed as output.

To verify that this solution algorithm is correct, we first build a table showing the required storage locations. Each column in the table indicates the content of one of the locations (see Figure 7-2). Entries will be made in the columns when the location contents change.

The rows of the table correspond to processing steps of the solution algorithm in which the content of any storage location may change. For convenience, the processing steps on the program flowchart are numbered in the same manner as the table (see Figure 7-1). The letter k is printed in each column of the first row of the table. This reminds us that each storage location contains something when program execution begins, although this program itself will not have caused anything to be placed there. Some of the processing steps may not be executed. Whether or not the conditional branches of the IFTHENELSEs are taken will depend on the outcomes of the comparison operations, or tests. These in turn depend on the input values.

Next, we build a table of input values. Since four values are required for one execution of this program, a table showing four values is sufficient. A table containing four values chosen at random is shown in Figure 7-3.

Having constructed these two tables, we are ready to simulate a program run. The steps in the simulated run are described as follows:

(a) The four input values are read into locations A, B, C, and D respectively. This is recorded in row 1 of the table as shown.

	A	B	C	D	Q
START	k	k	k	k	k
1	493	.06	5	.015	

(b) The value of A (493) is assigned to Q. This change in the content of Q is recorded in row 2 of the table.
(c) The value of Q (493) is compared to B (.06) at the first IFTHENELSE step. Since Q is greater than B, a branch occurs. The value of B is assigned to Q because we are looking for the smallest number. This change is recorded in row 3 of the table.
(d) The value of Q (.06) is compared to C (5). Since Q is not greater than B, no branch occurs. No change occurs at 4, so row 4 is deleted from the table.
(e) The value of Q (.06) is compared to D (.015). Since Q is greater than D, a branch occurs. The value of D is assigned to Q, and this change is recorded in row 5 of the table.
(f) The value of Q (.015) is provided as output.

	A	B	C	D	Q
START	k	k	k	k	k
1	493	.06	5	.015	
2					493
3					.06
4					
5					.015

Now look at the four input values (see Figure 7-3). Which value is smallest? Was the smallest value provided as output? Since .015 is smallest and was provided as output, the logic depicted by the program flowchart appears to be correct. To

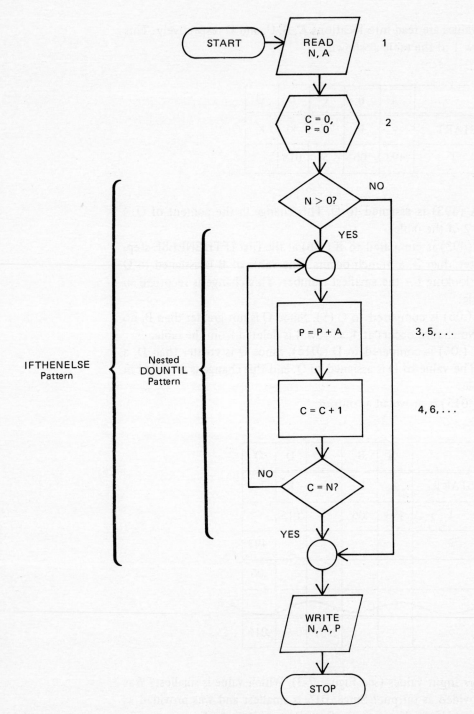

Figure 7-4

check, a second set of values should be chosen and processed in the same manner. (See Exercise 3.)

You may consider this sort of simulation to be an extremely detailed, time-consuming method of verification. It's true that preparing for and participating in a design review is not a simple task. But time and effort expended at this stage in program development are well spent. Care taken at this point can prevent or eliminate needless errors. The programmer may save many hours of programming time and avoid countless frustrations that might otherwise occur.

SAMPLE PROBLEM 7.1

Problem: Students at Garnel Business School are learning to use computers to solve both simple and complex problems. To insure that available computer time is used wisely, to encourage error-free coding, and to provide opportunities for students to learn from one another, each project is subjected to either informal or formal reviews throughout its development cycle. Figure 7-4 shows a program flowchart for the initial project of one of the students. Assume you are a member of the review team responsible for checking this solution algorithm.

Solution: The program flowchart in Figure 7-4 indicates that storage locations for the variables N, A, C, and P are needed in this solution algorithm. Values for two of the variables, N and A, are read as input. The others, C and P, are used as a loop control variable and an accumulator, respectively. Since N controls the number of times the program loop will be executed, and the value for N is provided as input, it is not known beforehand how many times the program loop will be executed and,

Table of Storage Locations

	N	A	C	P
START				
1				
2				

Figure 7-5

Table of Input Values

Location to Receive Data	Input Value
N	
A	

Figure 7-6

	N	A	C	P
START	k	k	k	k
1	2	75		
2			0	0
3				75
4			1	
5				150
6			2	

Figure 7-7

therefore, how many times the contents of the storage locations may change. Figures 7-5 and 7-6 show the general forms of the storage-locations and input-values tables needed to verify this solution algorithm.

The first question we might ask is whether this flowchart is a plan for a well-structured program. Do you see numerous examples of SIMPLE SEQUENCE, an IFTHENELSE, and a nested DOUNTIL? Since the DOUNTIL is a trailing-decision loop, we know that the steps in the loop will be executed at least once. How has the student programmer provided for the possibility that even this one execution should not occur? Since each processing step on the flowchart is part of a basic pattern or a combination thereof, we can conclude that the flowchart is a plan for a structured program.

But will it provide correct results? Assume the values 2 and 75 are provided as input. Perform a simulation, or procedure execution. When you have finished, your tables should look like the tables in Figures 7-7 and 7-8.

What were the original input values? How many times was the program loop executed? What values were provided as output? Observe that the algorithm adds a number to itself repetitively $(A + A + A + \ldots)$. It finds the value of N As, or $N \times A$. In this case, $75 + 75 = 150$, or $2 \times 75 = 150$. In other words, the algorithm accomplishes multiplication.

Usually you will be told beforehand what problem a program is to solve. We didn't state the problem in this example, to help insure that you did not read any logic into the algorithm that is not there—to give you experience in following each pro-

Location to Receive Data	Input Value
N	2
A	75

Figure 7-8

cessing step of a solution algorithm exactly as it is specified. Match your findings against the problem statement below:

A pair of positive values is to be read as input. The two values and their product are to be written as output.

A more specific problem statement, for which the same solution algorithm is applicable, is given below:

Bernal Supermarket maintains its special-order shelf inventory in a relatively small supply room adjacent to its receiving dock. For rough estimating purposes, the number of cases (N) of a received item is to be multiplied by the anticipated sales price per case (A) to determine the in-stock value of each addition to inventory. The number of cases, price, and in-stock value are to be printed as output.

On some computers, a multiplication operation can be performed directly because it is built into the computer as hardwired circuitry. On others, multiplication is available through special instructions known as **microcode,** which are placed in a **read-only storage (ROS)** unit of the computer before processing is initiated. (Instructions placed in ROS can be executed, but they cannot be deleted or changed.) On still others, multiplication must be performed by repeated addition, as specified in this solution algorithm. As noted earlier in this lesson, there may be several possible solutions to a problem, and it's important to find one that works well in a particular problem situation. An additional benefit of developing a generalized solution algorithm such as this one is that the algorithm may be useful in solving numerous, basically similar problems.

To complete this design verification, at least one additional pair of input values should be operated on, the steps of the solution algorithm should be traced again in detail, and the output produced should be compared against predetermined, correct results. (See Exercise 5.)

exercises

1. Express the solution algorithm represented by the program flowchart in Figure 7-1 in pseudocode form.
2. (a) Did you use a CASE control structure in your pseudocode representation of the solution algorithm?
   (b) Why is CASE appropriate, or inappropriate?
3. Assume the following values are provided as input to the program described in Figure 7-1: 25, 330, .35, and 102. They are to be assigned to the variables A, B, C, and D, respectively.
   (a) Construct a table of storage locations and a table of input values to be used in checking the solution algorithm, given these values as input.
   (b) Simulate the execution of the program, completing the table of storage locations by reflecting any contents changes as you proceed.
   (c) What value is provided as output of the program run?
   (d) What value should have been provided as output?
   (e) Do the results of your simulation uphold or refute the logic within the solution algorithm?
4. Express the solution algorithm for Sample Problem 7.1 (see Figure 7-4) in pseudocode form.
5. Assume the values 4 and 18 are provided as input for N and A, respectively, to the program-flowchart representation of the solution algorithm for Sample Problem 7.1.
   (a) Construct a table of storage locations and a table of input values to use in checking the algorithm, given these input values.
   (b) Simulate the execution of the program, completing the table of storage locations by reflecting any contents changes as you proceed.
   (c) What values are provided as output of the program run?
   (d) What values should have been provided as output?
6. Repeat Exercise 5, but check the pseudocode representation of the solution algorithm that you constructed in response to Exercise 4 rather than the program flowchart.
7. Construct a program flowchart or use pseudocode to show the processing steps needed to solve the following problem: Data items to be added are provided as input. The number of items to be added will be indicated by the first value provided as input (which is not to be included in the sum). A count of the number of data items whose values exceed 30,000 is also to be accumulated. The sum of the values added and the count of those exceeding 30,000 are to be provided as output. Be sure to plan a well-structured program.

8. Assume the following data items are to be added by the program that you planned in response to Exercise 7:

    44,316   203,667   15,550   430   30,000

    Create a table of all input to be provided to the program. Remember to include the input value needed to control end-of-file processing.

9. List the variables that identify storage locations required in the program that you planned in response to Exercise 7 as column headings in a table of storage locations. Perform a procedure execution to complete the table, showing the contents of the storage locations and any changes that occur.

10. What values are provided as output of the procedure execution in Exercise 9?

11. As a check, perform manually the calculations described in Exercise 7, on the data listed in Exercise 8, plus the necessary control value. Your answers should match those provided as output (see Exercise 10). If they do not, examine both your solution algorithm and your procedure execution to determine where errors have been made.

12. Construct a program flowchart or use pseudocode to show the processing steps needed to solve the following problem: Two data items, UPPER and LOWER, are to be read as input. The sum of all odd numbers from LOWER to UPPER, inclusive, is to be computed and printed. Assume that LOWER is less than UPPER. Be sure to plan a well-structured program.

13. Perform a procedure execution (including construction of the tables needed) of the solution algorithm that you constructed in response to Exercise 12, to answer the following questions:

    (a) What value is provided as output by the algorithm if LOWER is 3 and UPPER is 18?

    (b) Is the output of the algorithm correct?

    If the output is not correct, examine both your solution algorithm and your procedure execution to determine where errors have occurred.

14. Repeat Exercise 13, but assume that LOWER is 3 and UPPER is 4.

RELATING DESIGN AND CODE

After the solution algorithm has been verified in its design-language form, the actual writing of the program can begin. In some instances, all work up to this point will have been handled by a person employed as a **designer**, who will simply give the completed design documentation (say, the program flowchart or pseudocode) to another person who works as a **coder**. More commonly, a designer develops the high-level design documentation (such as the system flowchart), but both the detailed design work as we have discussed it and the writing of the program are done by a person employed as a **programmer**. Writing the program is stating the algorithm in a particular language, or **code**, so programming may also be called **coding**. We shall use the words *programming* and *coding,* and the words *programming language* and *code,* interchangeably.

Writing a program is the process of expressing the design-language representation of the solution algorithm in a programming-language form. This process is a rigorous one, because the programmer must follow very specific rules. Only certain characters from an allowable character set can be used; periods or semicolons (depending on the language) must be included as delimiters; the parameters of a statement must be specified in a certain positional order; and so on. The ease with which this task can be accomplished depends on several factors: the programmer's familiarity with the design language employed, the level of detail in the design documentation, the programmer's knowledge of the programming language to be used in coding, the suitability of that language to the problem-solving task, and so on. Many of these factors are beyond the scope of this book, but they must be taken into account within the overall program-development cycle.

Before writing statements about how input data will be received, the programmer should refer to, or create, **layout specifications** for the data. **A multiple-card layout**

form, which helps the programmer to visualize and keep in mind the locations of data items on 80-column punched cards, may be useful (see Figure 8-1). Similar forms are available for describing data on 96-column punched cards, magnetic tape, magnetic disk, and so on.

Before writing statements about how output data will be formatted, the programmer should refer to, or create, additional layout specifications. **Print charts** like the one shown in Figure 8-2 are commonly used. Forms that help to show the layout of data on the televisionlike screen of a visual-display unit are also available.

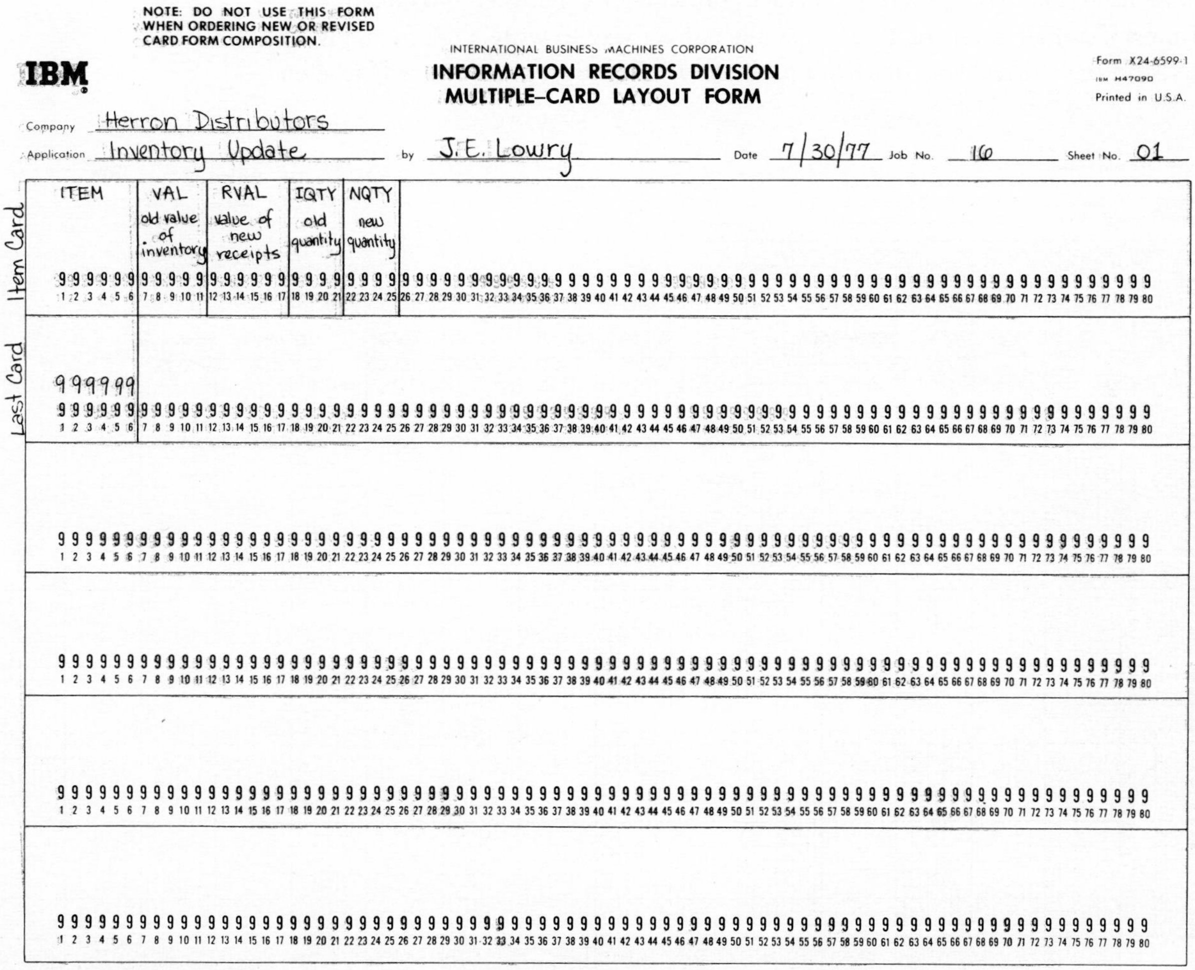

Figure 8-1

Careful planning and documentation of input/output formats helps to prevent coding errors. And we see here again, the importance of design documents as communication vehicles. The persons responsible for creating the input should verify that it will be in the form expected by the programmer. The persons who will receive the output should verify that it will contain the information they need, in a form that is convenient for them. In some cases, the input to one program is the output from another program in the application system. Perhaps the output from this program is to be used as input to a succeeding program. In either of these cases, correct and complete descriptions of input and output provide a basis for effective communication between programmers (and, subsequently, between programs).

In most if not all instances, there is no one correct way to write a program, just as there is no one correct way to solve a problem. Different programmers will develop

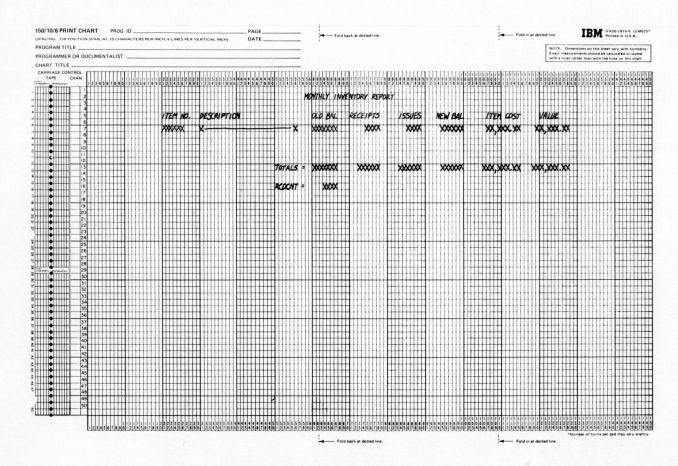

Figure 8-2

different sequences of instructions to perform a given series of operations, just as they will develop different solution algorithms for a problem. At this stage, the solution algorithm may have to be altered slightly to agree with machine logic or with techniques available in a selected programming language. Such changes should be minimal, but if required, they must be reflected in the design documentation. Then the solution algorithm, in its design-language form, should be re-verified.

In this book, the importance of planning a well-structured program is emphasized. As you might expect, some programming languages are better suited to structured programming than others. Most languages were defined and standardized according to recommendations of the American National Standards Institute (ANSI), before structured programming received widespread attention. A primary coding consideration is whether or not programming-language statements directly analogous to the control structures we have described are available in a particular language. If not, the programmer must use statements that are available in the language in ways that set up the control structures required.

Most of you will be writing programs in FORTRAN, COBOL, PL/I, or BASIC, so we shall direct our attention here to these languages. Look at Figure 8-3. The structured-programming control structures discussed in preceding lessons are expressed in pseudocode form in the left-hand column of this figure. Analogous general forms for FORTRAN, COBOL, PL/I, and BASIC are shown in the remaining columns of the chart. Most programmers who are writing structured programs establish general forms like these as patterns, or models—guides to refer to when writing structured code.

Of these languages, computer professionals generally agree that PL/I is most suitable for structured programming. It provides directly for the SIMPLE SEQUENCE, IFTHENELSE, and DOWHILE patterns and readily simulates DOUNTIL and CASE. The COBOL programmer makes frequent use of PERFORM statements in simulating control structures in COBOL programs. The FORTRAN programmer may need to include numerous logical IF and GO TO statements to set up required control structures. At the same time, the programmer must be careful to avoid using IF and GO TO statements, in any of the wide variety of forms available in FORTRAN, in an undisciplined manner. A similar situation exists when BASIC is used: IF and GO TO statements are needed to set up structured-programming control structures, but they should not be used for random branching in a program.

As we move from the design-language representation of a solution algorithm to program coding, let us start with a very simple example. Assume that an extensive amount of weather data has been collected for each month of the preceding year for weather analysis and weather prediction. The data includes maximum, minimum, and average records for temperature, humidity, and precipitation, totals for each of these, and so on. The data is stored on various magnetic-tape files.

Pseudocode		BASIC	FORTRAN

SIMPLE SEQUENCE

Pseudocode		BASIC	FORTRAN
s1		statement-s1	statement-s1
s2		statement-s2	statement-s2

IFTHENELSE

Pseudocode		BASIC	FORTRAN
IF cond THEN		IF not cond THEN 400	IF (not cond) GO TO 400
s1		REM THEN CLAUSE (OPTIONAL COMMENT)	statement-s1
ELSE		statement-s1	GO TO 500
s2		GO TO 500	400 CONTINUE
ENDIF		REM ELSE CLAUSE (OPTIONAL COMMENT)	statement-s2
	400	statement-s2	500 CONTINUE
	500	...	

CASE

Pseudocode		BASIC	FORTRAN
CASENTRY selection		ON exp GO TO sn1,sn2,...,snn	GO TO (sn1,sn2,...,snn) var
CASE 1	sn1	REM CASE 1 (OPTIONAL COMMENT)	Exception routine
Case-c1 function		Case-c1 function	GO TO 990
CASE 2		GO TO 990	sn1 CONTINUE
Case-c2 function	sn2	REM CASE 2 (OPTIONAL COMMENT)	Case-c1 function
.		Case-c2 function	GO TO 990
.		GO TO 990	sn2 CONTINUE
.		.	Case-c2 function
CASE n		.	GO TO 990
Case-cn function		.	.
ENDCASE	snn	REM CASE N (OPTIONAL COMMENT)	.
		Case-cn function	.
		GO TO 990	snn CONTINUE
		REM END CASE (OPTIONAL COMMENT)	Case-cn function
	990	...	GO TO 990
			990 CONTINUE

DOWHILE

Pseudocode		BASIC	FORTRAN
DOWHILE cond		REM DOWHILE (OPTIONAL COMMENT)	200 CONTINUE
s1	200	IF not cond THEN 300	IF (not cond) GO TO 300
ENDDO		statement-s1	statement-s1
		GO TO 200	GO TO 200
	300	...	300 CONTINUE

DOUNTIL

Pseudocode		BASIC	FORTRAN
DOUNTIL cond		REM DOUNTIL (OPTIONAL COMMENT)	200 CONTINUE
s1	200	statement-s1	statement-s1
ENDDO		IF not cond THEN 200	IF (not cond) GO TO 200

Note: For clarity, statement numbers other than those used in the control structures are not shown in these BASIC examples.

Figure 8-3

COBOL	PL/I	Pseudocode

SIMPLE SEQUENCE

```
COBOL:
statement-s1.
statement-s2.

PL/I:
statement_s1;
statement_s2;

Pseudocode:
s1
s2
```

IFTHENELSE

```
COBOL:
IF cond
   statement-s1
ELSE
   statement-s2.

PL/I:
IF cond THEN
   statement_s1;
ELSE
   statement_s2;

Pseudocode:
IF cond THEN
   s1
ELSE
   s2
ENDIF
```

CASE

```
COBOL:
   PERFORM CASE-STRUC THRU END-CASE.
   .
   .
   .
CASE-STRUC.
   GO TO CASE1,CASE2,...,CASEN
      DEPENDING ON identifier.
      Exception routine.
      GO TO END-CASE.
CASE1.
   Case-c1 function.
   GO TO END-CASE.
CASE2.
   Case-c2 function.
   GO TO END-CASE.
   .
   .
CASEN.
   Case-cn function.
   GO TO END-CASE.
END-CASE.
   EXIT.

PL/I:
   DCL CASE(1:N) LABEL
       INIT (CASE1,CASE2,...,CASEN),
       MAXCASE FIXED BIN (15) INIT (N);
   ON CONDITION (CASERANGE)
      on-unit action;
      .
      .
      .
   INCASE = integer_expression;
   IF INCASE < 1 | INCASE > MAXCASE THEN
      SIGNAL CONDITION (CASERANGE);
   ELSE;
      GO TO CASE (INCASE);
CASE1: DO;
      Case_c1 function;
      GO TO CASE_END;
   END;
CASE2: DO;
      Case_c2 function;
      GO TO CASE_END;
   END;
      .
      .
CASEN: DO;
      Case-cn function;
      GO TO CASE_END;
   END;
CASE_END:;

Pseudocode:
CASENTRY selection
   CASE 1
      Case-c1 function
   CASE 2
      Case-c2 function
      .
      .
      .
   CASE n
      Case-cn function
ENDCASE
```

DOWHILE

```
COBOL:
PERFORM S1
   UNTIL not cond.

PL/I:
DO WHILE (cond);
   statement_s1;
END;

Pseudocode:
DOWHILE cond
   s1
ENDDO
```

DOUNTIL

```
COBOL:
PERFORM S1.
PERFORM S1
   UNTIL cond.

PL/I:
DCL TESTV BIT (1);
   .
   .
   .
TESTV = '1'B;
DO WHILE (TESTV);
   statement_s1;
   IF cond THEN
      TESTV = '0'B;
   ELSE;
END;

Pseudocode:
DOUNTIL cond
   s1
ENDDO
```

Figure 8-3 (continued)

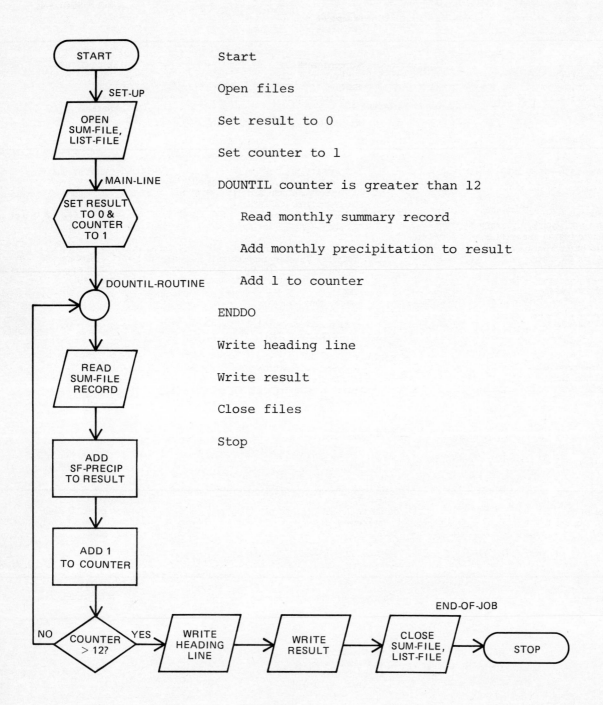

Start

Open files

Set result to 0

Set counter to 1

DOUNTIL counter is greater than 12

    Read monthly summary record

    Add monthly precipitation to result

    Add 1 to counter

ENDDO

Write heading line

Write result

Close files

Stop

Figure 8-4

A program is needed to read one of the files, a summary file (SUM-FILE) containing one record for each month of the year. The program is to extract the total monthly precipitation figure from each record and accumulate a total annual precipitation figure. When all 12 records have been read, a heading line that identifies the output, and a detail line giving the name of the file from which the data was extracted (SUM-FILE) and the total annual precipitation figure are to be printed on an output file (LIST-FILE). The program is to be written in COBOL.

An algorithm for a well-structured program to accomplish this processing is shown in program-flowchart form at the left in Figure 8-4. The same algorithm is expressed in pseudocode form at the right. The COBOL representation of the algorithm is given in Figure 8-5. We see here the Procedure Division of a COBOL program. Since this is the division of a COBOL program that contains the procedural steps of the solution algorithm, it is the part of the program that we are most interested in at present. For brevity, the Identification, Environment, and Data Divisions of the program are not included in this book. But those of you who are studying COBOL or are familiar with it are encouraged to complete appropriate coding for these divisions of the program.

```
PROCEDURE DIVISION.
SET-UP SECTION.
    OPEN INPUT SUM-FILE, OUTPUT LIST-FILE.
MAIN-LINE SECTION.
    MOVE ZEROS TO RESULT.
    MOVE 1 TO COUNTER.
    PERFORM DOUNTIL-ROUTINE.
    PERFORM DOUNTIL-ROUTINE UNTIL COUNTER > 12.
    MOVE HDG-LINE TO PRINT-AREA.
    WRITE PRINT-AREA AFTER ADVANCING 2 LINES.
    MOVE RESULT TO LIST-RESULT.
    MOVE SF-NAME TO LIST-NAME.
    MOVE DETAIL-LINE TO PRINT-AREA.
    WRITE PRINT-AREA AFTER ADVANCING 2 LINES.
END-OF-JOB SECTION.
    CLOSE SUM-FILE, LIST-FILE.
    STOP RUN.
DOUNTIL-ROUTINE.
    READ SUM-FILE RECORD.
    ADD SF-PRECIP TO RESULT.
    ADD 1 TO COUNTER.
```

Figure 8-5

We can readily recognize several SIMPLE SEQUENCE patterns and a DOUNTIL control structure in the design-language representations of the solution algorithm in Figure 8-4. Remember that the DOUNTIL control structure is a trailing-decision loop. The test for the loop terminating condition is not made until the other processing steps in the loop have been executed. So we always perform the processing steps in the loop at least once.

Since there is no DOUNTIL statement in COBOL, we simulate the DOUNTIL control structure by means of PERFORM statements. The first PERFORM insures that the processing steps in the loop (the DOUNTIL routine in Figure 8-5) are executed at least once. To understand why this is necessary, you need to know that the succeeding PERFORM with the UNTIL clause sets up a leading-decision loop, the DOWHILE pattern of structured programming. Whether or not the DOUNTIL routine is executed again depends upon whether the loop control variable COUNTER is greater than 12. (Remember that a DOUNTIL control structure is really a convenient way of expressing a SIMPLE SEQUENCE pattern followed by a DOWHILE pattern as shown in Figure 6-1. The general form for the COBOL representation of a DOUNTIL control structure is given as the last entry in the COBOL column in Figure 8-3.)

You should verify that the program flowchart, pseudocode, and COBOL representations of this solution algorithm (Figures 8-4 and 8-5) are equivalent. **Cross-references** have been included on the flowchart in Figure 8-4 to help point out the correspondence between steps on the flowchart and statements in the COBOL program. Each cross reference is the label of a section or paragraph in the COBOL program. (ANSI recommends that cross references be placed to the upper right of flowcharting symbols, as in Figure 8-4.) By adding cross references to a flowchart, the programmer makes it easier for others to follow the logic in the program.

Now let's look at another example. A basic read-and-print program is needed in most business data-processing environments. It can be used to create highly readable summary reports of data stored in computer files, display the contents of input transactions for verification purposes, build parts catalogs, create mailing labels, generate address lists, create internal telephone directories, and so on. An algorithm for a well-structured basic read-and-print program is shown in flowchart form in Figure 8-6 and in pseudocode in Figure 8-7. A computer-program representation of the algorithm, written in FORTRAN, is shown in Figure 8-8.

Both the program flowchart and the pseudocode representation of the algorithm show that a DOWHILE pattern and a nested IFTHENELSE are needed. There are numerous examples of SIMPLE SEQUENCE as well.

The DOWHILE pattern in the FORTRAN program is introduced by the comment BEGIN DOWHILE and implemented through use of a logical IF statement. The nested IFTHENELSE is also set up by a logical IF. (To review the general forms for

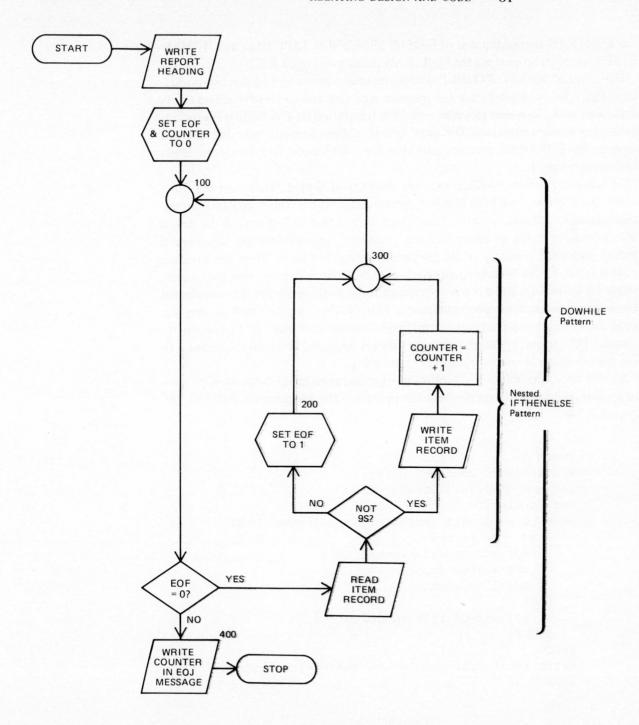

Figure 8-6

the FORTRAN representations of SIMPLE SEQUENCE, DOWHILE, and IFTHEN-ELSE control structures, see the FORTRAN column of Figure 8-3.)

The frequent use of CONTINUE statements as shown in Figure 8-8 is not mandatory, but it helps to emphasize the program structure and to prevent coding errors associated with the points to which control is transferred. It also facilitates program debugging and maintenance. The same is true of the comment lines. Indention is used in the FORTRAN program, just as in the pseudocode, to indicate the levels of nesting required.

As suggested for the COBOL example above, you should verify that the flowchart, pseudocode, and FORTRAN representations of this solution algorithm are equivalent. In common practice, this check of program coding against the design documentation helps to insure that the previously verified solution algorithm is indeed expressed correctly in its programming-language form. Then the program coding (after having been keypunched, if necessary) must be submitted to the computer for translation into a machine-language form. This translation is accomplished by a language-translator program (here a FORTRAN compiler) that accepts the program as input and produces the machine-language equivalent of that coding as output. The output, commonly called an **object program**, can then be loaded into computer storage to control subsequent processing.

At this time, the solution algorithm in its machine-language form must be verified. This verification is performed by executing the program on test data. As

```
Start
Write report heading
Set end-of-file indicator to 0
Set counter to 0
DOWHILE more data (end-of-file indicator = 0)
   Read item record
   IF not end-of-file record THEN
      write item record
      add 1 to counter
   ELSE
      set end-of-file indicator to 1
   ENDIF
ENDDO
Write total from counter in end-of-job message
Stop
```

Figure 8-7

described for design verification in Lesson 7, actual outputs should be compared against predetermined, correct results. The cause of any discrepancies must be determined. Once again, the design documentation comes in handy. The programmer can refer to the flowchart or pseudocode, for example, to manually trace the operations performed on the test data values. Doing so often helps the programmer to determine where errors have occurred. If any changes are made to the solution algorithm at this time, they should be reflected not only in the program coding but also in the design documentation. The solution algorithm, in its revised form, should be re-verified.

```
C          FORTRAN PRINTOUT OF ITEM CARDS FOR VERIFICATION PURPOSES
           INTEGER ITEM, NUM, DES(68), EOF, COUNT
           WRITE (3,20)
    20     FORMAT (16X, 'PRINTOUT OF ITEM CARDS'///3X, 'ITEM NO.',
           14X, 'QUANTITY', 8X, 'DESCRIPTION'/)
           EOF = 0
           COUNT = 0
C          BEGIN DOWHILE
   100     CONTINUE
           IF (EOF.NE.0) GO TO 400
               READ (1,120) ITEM, NUM, DES
   120         FORMAT (I6,I6,17A4)
C          BEGIN NESTED IFTHENELSE
           IF (ITEM.EQ.999999) GO TO 200
C          BEGIN THEN OF NESTED IFTHENELSE
               WRITE (3,130) ITEM, NUM, DES
   130         FORMAT (5X,I6,6X,I6,4X,17A4)
               COUNT = COUNT + 1
               GO TO 300
C          BEGIN ELSE OF NESTED IFTHENELSE
   200         CONTINUE
               EOF = 1
   300         CONTINUE
           GO TO 100
   400     CONTINUE
C          END-OF-JOB PROCESSING
           WRITE (3,420) COUNT
   420     FORMAT ('1END OF JOB; NUMBER OF RECORDS = ',I4)
           STOP
           END
```

Figure 8-8

SAMPLE PROBLEM 8.1

Problem: The research chemists at Singleton Labs make widespread use of a mathematical approach to problem-solving, commonly known as the **quadratic equation**. In its most general form, this equation is expressed as

$$ax^2 + bx + c = 0$$

where a, b, and c are constants directly related to the problem to be solved. Once a chemist has determined a, b, and c for a particular problem (as given in the problem statement or determined directly from it), the next step is to find the x values, or **roots**, that satisfy the equation above. These roots can be computed using the **quadratic formula**, which is expressed in its general form as

$$x = \frac{-b \pm \sqrt{b^2 - 4ac}}{2a}$$

Because this computation is needed so frequently, may involve very large or very small numbers, and must be done correctly, one of the chemists recommended using a computer. A simple, general-purpose PL/I program is to be written to direct the computer in finding the acceptable x values.

Solution: A plan for the solution to this problem—that is, for finding the roots of a quadratic equation—is shown in Figures 8-9 and 8-10. Here, we see the quadratic formula implemented as a sequence of algorithmic steps, described in both flowchart and pseudocode forms.

A nested IFTHENELSE pattern provides the basic structure within this solution algorithm. There are, of course, numerous examples of SIMPLE SEQUENCE as well.

The variables A, B, and C correspond directly to the constants a, b, and c in the quadratic formula. The values for these variables are read as input primarily to provide flexibility: the algorithm that is actually set up during exeution can include any of a wide variety of values for A, B, and C. But, once these values are read, they are not changed during execution of the algorithm, so they are in effect constants within the problem-solving task.

Note that we check first to insure that A is not equal to 0, because if A were 0, then the divisor 2A would be 0, and division by 0 yields unpredictable results.

The variable D represents the **discriminant** (a mathematical term used for $b^2 - 4ac$). Because we are only interested in **real roots** of the equation, if there are any, we check next to insure that the discriminant is greater than zero. The roots will be real if and only if this condition is true. (Otherwise, our computation would involve finding the square root of a negative value.) If the discriminant is not greater than

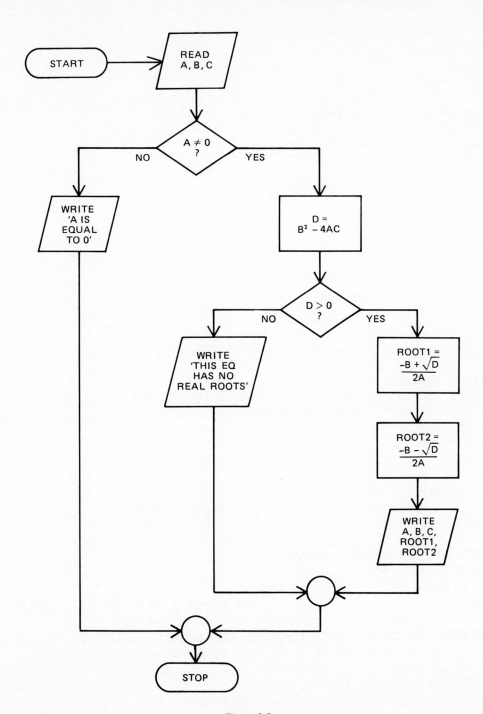

Figure 8-9

```
Start
Read A, B, C
IF A is not equal to 0 THEN
    D = B² - 4AC
    IF D is greater than 0 THEN
        find ROOT1:  (-B + √D) / 2A
        find ROOT2:  (-B - √D) / 2A
        write A, B, C, ROOT1, ROOT2
    ELSE
        write 'THIS EQUATION HAS NO REAL ROOTS'
    ENDIF
ELSE
    write 'A IS EQUAL TO 0'
ENDIF
Stop
```

Figure 8-10

```
SQROOT:  PROC OPTIONS (MAIN);
/* THIS PROGRAM FINDS THE REAL ROOTS OF A QUADRATIC EQUATION */
        DCL A, B, C, D, ROOT1, ROOT2 DEC FLOAT;
LGET:    GET LIST (A, B, C);
        IF A ¬ = 0   THEN
            DO;                                 /* BLOCK 1  */
            D = (B * B) - (4 * A * C);
            IF D > 0 THEN
                DO;                             /* BLOCK 2  */
                SQRD = SQRT (D);
                DIV = 2 * A;
                ROOT1 = (-B + SQRD) / (DIV) ;
                ROOT2 = (-B - SQRD) / (DIV) ;
                PUT LIST (A, B, C, ROOT1, ROOT2);
                END;                            /* BLOCK 2 */
            ELSE
                PUT LIST (A, B, C, 'THIS EQUATION HAS NO REAL ROOTS');
            END;                                /* BLOCK 1 */
        ELSE
            PUT LIST ('A IS EQUAL TO 0');
        END;                                    /* SQROOT  */
```

Figure 8-11

zero, we simply write a message indicating that there are no real roots and terminate processing.

The PL/I implementation of this algorithm is shown in Figure 8-11. Note that the statements within the THEN clause of the outer IFTHENELSE pattern are bounded by the DO and END statements of a PL/I DO group. These DO and END statements cause all statements within the group to be treated as a single statement, or block (referred to as BLOCK 1 in the program comments). The THEN clause of the inner IFTHENELSE pattern is set up in a similar manner (BLOCK 2). The PL/I SQRT built-in function is used to find the real roots, provided that A is not equal to 0 and D is greater than 0, as specified in the program design. The comments, indentions, and meaningful variable names, and the printed output documentation, help us to understand the problem-solving steps of the solution algorithm. (To review the general forms for the PL/I representations of SIMPLE SEQUENCE and IFTHENELSE control structures, look at the first and second descriptions in the PL/I column of Figure 8-3.)

exercises

1. Distinguish between the work of a coder and that of a programmer.
2. Describe two program design tools available to the programmer for planning the formats of input and output.
3. Describe a situation where the design-language representation of a solution algorithm has to be re-verified.
4. What does the phrase "simulate the DOUNTIL control structure" mean, say, when writing a COBOL program?
5. Support or refute the following statement: "A GO TO statement should not be used in a well-structured program."
6. (a) What are cross-references on a program flowchart?
   (b) How are they used?
7. Use either pseudocode or flowcharting symbols to plan the portions of program logic specified below.
   (a) Values for RATE and TIME are to be read as input. RATE is to be multiplied by TIME to determine DISTANCE. RATE, TIME, and DISTANCE are to be written as output.
   (b) As in 7(a), but the processing steps are to be repeated until six pairs of input values have been processed.
   (c) As in 7(a), but the multiplication and output operations are to occur only if RATE exceeds 60.

8. Refer to the general forms for structured-programming control structures in Figure 8-3 and language texts or reference manuals of your choice (or as specified by your instructor) to write programming-language representations of the program logic that you planned for Exercise 7.

9. Use a programming language other than COBOL to express the solution algorithm represented in Figures 8-4 and 8-5.

10. Use a programming language other than FORTRAN to express the solution algorithm shown in Figures 8-6 through 8-8.

11. Use a programming language other than PL/I to express the solution algorithm shown in Figures 8-9 through 8-11.

12. Construct a program flowchart or use pseudocode to show the processing steps needed to solve the following problem: High-dollar items of inventory are defined to be those items where quantity on hand times unit price equals or exceeds a dollar value established by plant inventory control management. The first record provided as input to an inventory control program will indicate the established high-dollar value. Each succeeding record will contain the item number, quantity on hand, and unit price of an item in inventory. The program should print out the item number of each item that exceeds high-dollar value and indicate the amount by which this value is exceeded. Program execution should be terminated when a record containing item number 99999 is processed. Be sure to plan a well-structured program.

13. Perform a procedure execution (including construction of the tables needed) of the solution algorithm that you constructed in response to Exercise 12. Select five appropriate inputs (or use those specified by your instructor) and determine what the outputs should be beforehand, for verification purposes.

14. When you have completed Exercise 13 successfully, use a programming language of your choice (or as specified by your instructor) to express the verified solution algorithm in a computer-program form.

GROUPING DATA ITEMS

In preceding lessons we have directed our attention to the reading, processing, and writing of single values. Each value was stored in a particular location and referred to as a **single** (or **simple**) **variable**. For each such variable, we selected and used a particular variable name (COUNT, N, A, ITEM, NUM, and so on). This need not always be the case.

Suppose a list of 10 input values is to be read into 10 consecutive storage locations. We can assign a unique name to each of the 10 locations—say, INPUT1, INPUT2, and so on. We can use the names to refer to the values throughout the program.

But what if the list contained 100 or even 1000 values? The same approach might work, but it would certainly not be convenient. Writing the program would be a tedious, time-consuming chore. With so many different values and corresponding variable names to keep track of, errors would be apt to occur.

Suppose that, instead of treating the 10 input values as 10 similar but separate data items, we treat them as a group of data items. We reserve a storage area large enough for all of the values, and we assign a name to that area. Various terms are used to describe data items stored and identified in this way. In COBOL, this kind of data group is usually known as a **single-level table**; in FORTRAN, BASIC, or PL/I, it may be called a **list**, **vector**, or **one-dimensional array**.

Only the group of data items is given a name. An individual item in the group is referred to by stating its relative position (on a left-to-right basis). This position is specified by means of a **subscript** following the group name.[1]

---

1. In COBOL, a distinction exists between a **subscript**, which is an integer value ("occurrence number") that may range from 1 to the total number of entries in a table, and an **index**, which is a storage displacement value from the beginning of the table. In other programming languages, the terms *subscript* and *index* are used interchangeably with respect to the identification of data items in a group. In this discussion, the term *subscript* can be understood to mean either.

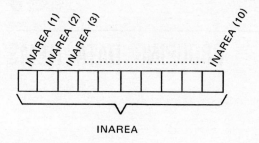

Figure 9-1

As an example, then, let us assume that a storage area is reserved for the 10 input values mentioned above and that the name INAREA is assigned to the area (see Figure 9-1). Use of the **unsubscripted variable** INAREA, if permitted in the programming language, is interpreted as a reference to all of the items in the group. Individual items in the group are referred by means of the **subscripted variables** INAREA(1), INAREA(2), and so on.

Grouping capabilities are available in numerous programming languages. Because it is to our advantage to make use of them, we shall examine the program logic needed to deal with grouped data items in this lesson.

Figure 9-2 shows the program logic required to read 20 values into 20 consecutive storage locations as a group. The group name is V, for **vector**. The letter K is used as a subscript to point to a particular **member** (or **element**) of the vector. When K is 1, the subscripted variable V(1) refers to the first element of the vector; when K is 2, the subscripted variable V(2) points to the second element; and so on. A DO-UNTIL loop is executed repetitively, with the value of K increased by 1 on each execution. The loop is exited when the value of K is equal to 20. At that time, all 20 values have been read into storage.

Assume that the flowchart in Figure 9-2 is the first page of a two-page flowchart. Our task is not finished when we have read the 20 values into storage. We haven't used any of them yet. Let us suppose that we are to find and print the smallest of the 20 values. Figure 9-3 is the second page of the flowchart. It shows how to accomplish this part of the task.

We begin our search for the smallest value by assuming arbitrarily that the first member of the vector V, which is V(1), holds the smallest value. We store this value in S, the location set aside for the smallest value.

The DOUNTIL control structure in Figure 9-3 controls subsequent processing. All succeeding members of V are compared with the value in S by means of the nested IFTHENELSE. Any value smaller than the current content of S becomes, itself, the current content of S, via the THEN clause (YES path) of the IFTHENELSE. The DOUNTIL loop is exited when K is equal to 20. At that time, the content of S is the smallest value. This value is written as output, and processing is terminated.

The value 20 used in this algorithm could easily be replaced by another value. This would permit us to handle other than 20 values and therefore to find the smallest value in a different-sized group of data items. Changes to the program flow-chart or pseudocode and to the programming-language representation of the algorithm would be minimal.

Even greater flexibility would be available if the number of values to be processed

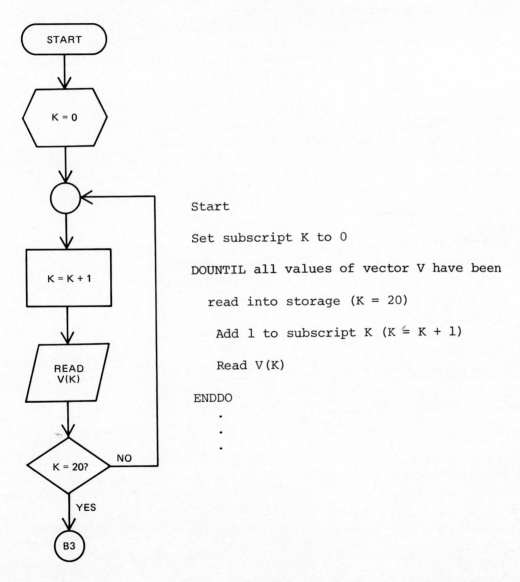

```
Start

Set subscript K to 0

DOUNTIL all values of vector V have been

    read into storage (K = 20)

    Add 1 to subscript K (K = K + 1)

    Read V(K)

ENDDO
    .
    .
    .
```

Figure 9-2

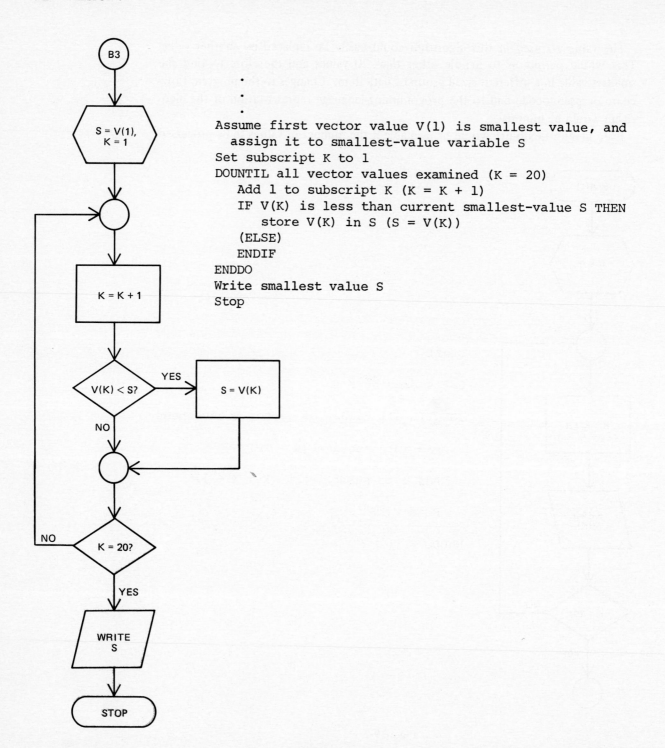

```
Assume first vector value V(1) is smallest value, and
   assign it to smallest-value variable S
Set subscript K to 1
DOUNTIL all vector values examined (K = 20)
   Add 1 to subscript K (K = K + 1)
   IF V(K) is less than current smallest-value S THEN
      store V(K) in S (S = V(K))
   (ELSE)
   ENDIF
ENDDO
Write smallest value S
Stop
```

Figure 9-3

were indicated by means of the first input value—a technique we have used earlier. This value could be assigned to a variable, say N, for use in loop control. The program could be used to find the smallest of any number of values without any program modification; only the first input value would have to be changed. (See Exercise 4.)

Sometimes the task of finding the smallest value of a set of values is the first step in placing the values in ascending sequence. A common method of sorting data into a required sequence is to read the values to be sorted into storage as a group of data items. One additional storage location, for use as a temporary storage area, is required. The value in the first position of the group is compared with the value in the next positon of the group. If the value in the first position is larger than the value in the second, they are interchanged. To perform this interchange, (1) the first value is placed in the temporary storage area; (2) the second value is transferred from its original position to the first value's original position; and (3) the first value is transferred from the temporary storage area to the second value's original position. This interchange is shown schematically in Figure 9-4.

After the values in positions 2, 3, 4, . . . , n have been compared with the value currently in the first position, the first pass through the values is complete. The first position of the group is definitely known to contain the smallest value.

This first position is then temporarily ignored. The value in the second position of the group is compared with each of the values in positions 3, 4, 5, . . . , n in a second pass. At the end of this pass, the second position is known to contain the second-to-smallest value.

The execution of passes continues, each pass requiring one less comparison

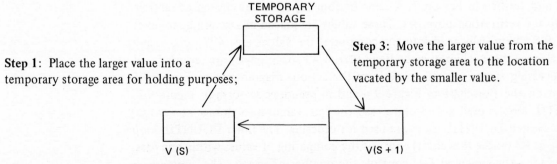

Step 1: Place the larger value into a temporary storage area for holding purposes;

Step 3: Move the larger value from the temporary storage area to the location vacated by the smaller value.

Step 2: Store the smaller value in the location that the larger value occupied; and

Figure 9-4

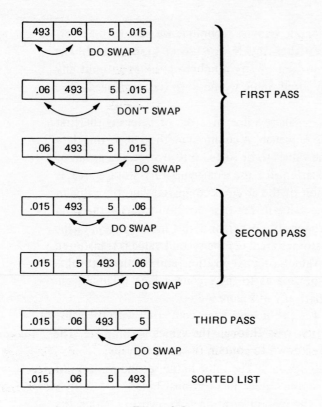

Figure 9-5

operation than the preceding pass. After n-1 passes, the values in the group are in ascending order.

For example, recall the algorithm to find the smallest of four numbers, which we discussed and verified in Lesson 7. A table of four input values chosen at random was set up for verification purposes. These values are placed in ascending sequence in Figure 9-5. As initially read into the computer, the values are: 493, .06, 5, and .015. To arrange these values in ascending order, 4 – 1, or 3, passes are required.

The processing steps required to perform the actions diagrammed in Figure 9-5 are shown on the flowchart in Figure 9-6 and in pseudocode form in Figure 9-7. A DOUNTIL loop is used as before to read the four values into storage as a group, or vector. Nested DOUNTIL loops are used for ordering. The inner DOUNTIL loop (beginning at B3 on the flowchart) controls the comparing of values within one pass. The outer loop (beginning at G1) controls the number of passes. The comparison is set up as an IFTHENELSE. This algorithm sorts only four values, but it demonstrates a technique that can be used to sort any number of values (see Exercise 8).

To refer to a specific element in any of the data groups discussed thus far, we have used a subscripted variable containing only a single subscript (INAREA(1),

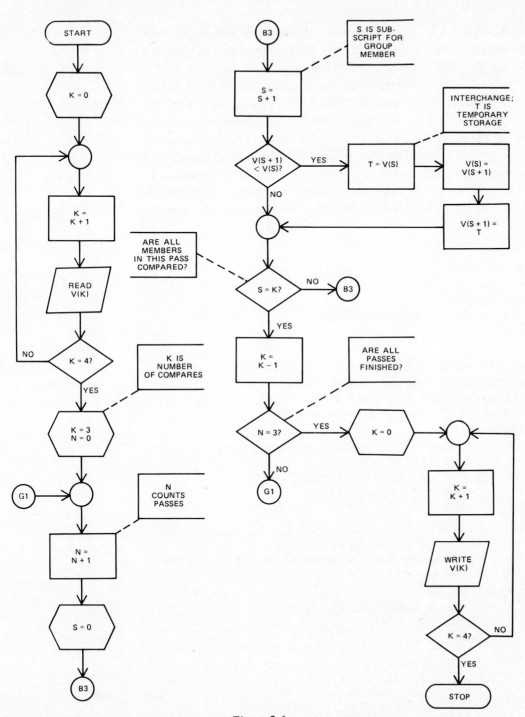

Figure 9-6

INAREA(2), V(S), where S = 1,2, . . ., n). One subscript was sufficient to identify a particular element because each group had a very simple structure. It could be treated as a list. We say that such a group has one **dimension**.

In some problem situations, it is convenient to treat a group of values as though it has more than one dimension. For example, instead of storing values as a list, we can store them as a table. Such a data group has two dimensions: **rows** and **columns**. A specific member of the group is identified by a subscripted variable having two subscripts. The first subscript identifies a particular row; the second identifies a particular column. Here again, the terminology used for the data group varies. In COBOL, this kind of group is called a **two-level**, or **multilevel**, **table**. In FORTRAN, BASIC, OR PL/I, it may be called a **table**, **matrix**, or **two-dimensional**, or **multi-dimensional**, **array**.

```
Start
Set subscript K to 0
DOUNTIL all values of vector V have been
  read into storage (K=4)
  Add 1 to subscript K (K = K + 1)
  Read V(K)
ENDDO
Set number of compares K to 3
Set count of passes N to 0
DOUNTIL all passes are finished (N = 3)
   Add 1 to count of passes N (N = N + 1)
   Set subscript S to 0
   DOUNTIL all members in this pass are compared (S=K)
   Add 1 to subscript S (S = S + 1)
      IF V(S+1) is less than V(S) THEN
         interchange V(S+1) and V(S)
      (ELSE)
      ENDIF
   ENDDO
   Subtract 1 from number of compares K (K = K - 1)
ENDDO
Set subscript K to 0
DOUNTIL all values of sorted vector V
  have been written out (K=4)
  Add 1 to subscript K (K = K + 1)
  Write V(K)
ENDDO
Stop
```

Figure 9-7

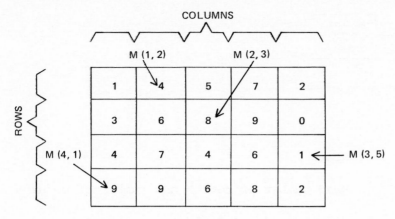

Figure 9-8

The table in Figure 9-8 contains numerical values. It has four rows and five columns. M is the name assigned to the table. Double-subscripted variables are used to refer to specific members of the table. For example, M(2,3) refers to the value in the second row and third column of the table, or 8. Similarly, M(4,1) refers to the value in the fourth row and first column, or 9. The number of rows times the number of columns (4 × 5, in this example) tells the total number of elements in the table.

The algorithm in Figure 9-9 reads values into consecutive storage locations as a two-dimensional group, Table A. The first pair of values submitted as input indicates the number of rows (M) and the number of columns (N) in the table. Specific members (elements) of the table are entered, **row by row**, one member at a time. All members of row 1 are read first, starting with the value in the first column and proceeding to the value in the last (Nth) column. Then all members of row 2 are read, and so on. Nested DOUNTIL loops are used to set up the processing logic required. The inner DOUNTIL loop controls the reading of values into specific columns; the outer DOUNTIL loop controls the row in which these columns are located.

After all members of the table have been read into storage (that is, both the inner DOUNTIL and the outer DOUNTIL have been exited), specific values from the table can be used in subsequent processing.

Assume that the problem to be solved requires that we read a second group of data items—a list having N elements. We are to multiply each element in every row of the table by the list element in the corresponding position. First, we multiply each element of the first row by each corresponding element of the list; then we multiply each element of the second row by each corresponding element of the list; and so on. The number of elements in the list must be the same as the number of

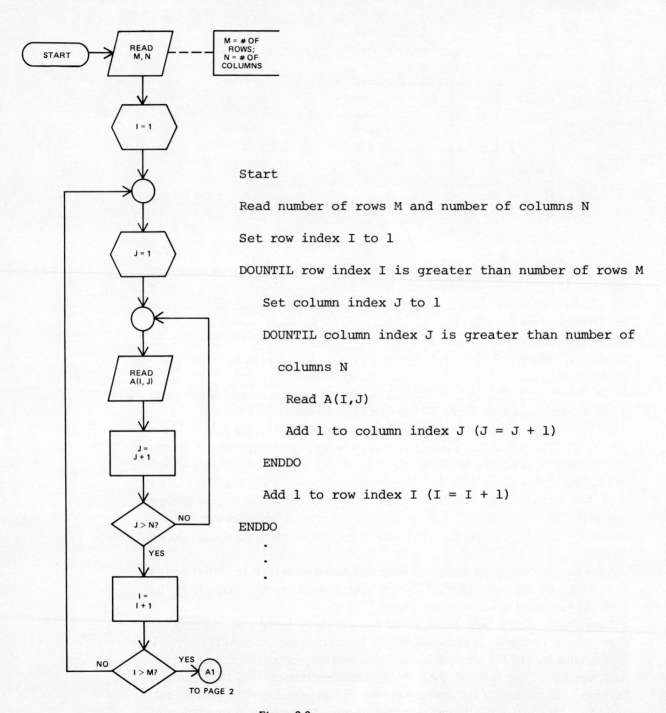

Start

Read number of rows M and number of columns N

Set row index I to 1

DOUNTIL row index I is greater than number of rows M

    Set column index J to 1

    DOUNTIL column index J is greater than number of

      columns N

        Read A(I,J)

        Add 1 to column index J (J = J + 1)

ENDDO

Add 1 to row index I (I = I + 1)

ENDDO

    .

    .

    .

Figure 9-9

columns in the table. As an example, assuming A is the table, and V is the list (or vector), we find

$$T(I, K) = A(I,K)*V(K)$$

repeatedly, with I ranging from 1 to the total number of rows (M) in the table, and K ranging from 1 to the total number of columns (N). In effect, a new two-dimensional group which we have called T is constructed, element by element. Its dimensions are the same as the dimensions of the original table, A, but its contents differ. Each value in T is the result of a multiplication operation.

Assume the flowchart in Figure 9-9 is page 1 of the flowchart for this algorithm. As we just discussed, it shows the reading of Table A. Figure 9-10 is page 2. It shows the reading of Vector V. The logic is also shown in pseudocode form. (Note the similarities and differences between this part of the algorithm and the logic in Figure 9-2.) Figure 9-11 is page 3. It shows the required multiplication and the printing of the new table, T. Documentation within the annotation symbols

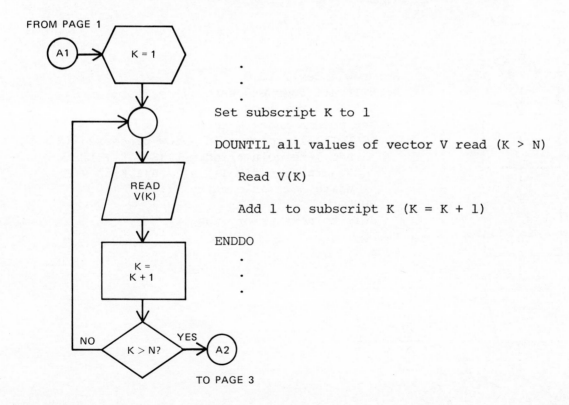

```
FROM PAGE 1

A1      K = 1

              .
              .
              .
        Set subscript K to 1

        DOUNTIL all values of vector V read (K > N)

READ        Read V(K)
V(K)
            Add 1 to subscript K (K = K + 1)

K =     ENDDO
K + 1         .
              .
              .

NO      YES
    K > N?    A2

        TO PAGE 3
```

Figure 9-10

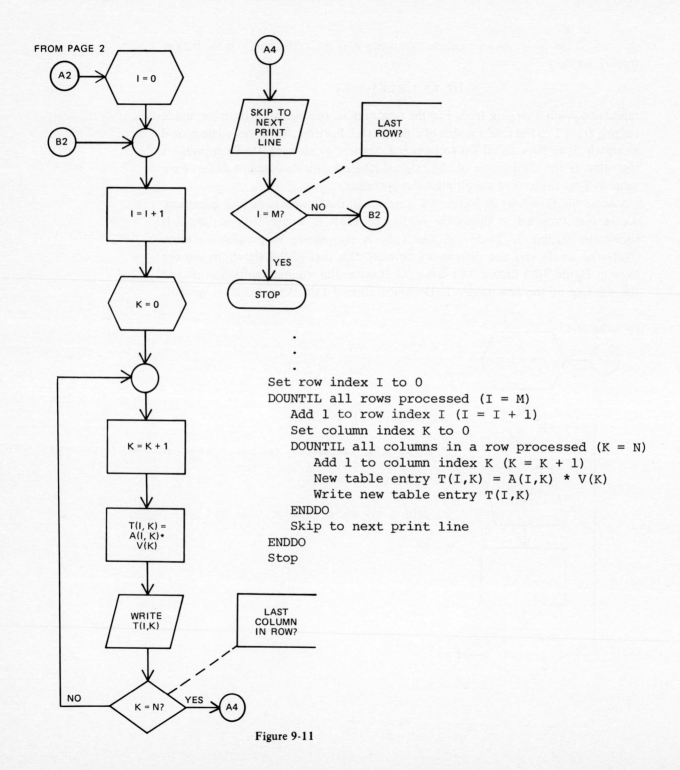

```
Set row index I to 0
DOUNTIL all rows processed (I = M)
    Add 1 to row index I (I = I + 1)
    Set column index K to 0
    DOUNTIL all columns in a row processed (K = N)
        Add 1 to column index K (K = K + 1)
        New table entry T(I,K) = A(I,K) * V(K)
        Write new table entry T(I,K)
    ENDDO
    Skip to next print line
ENDDO
Stop
```

Figure 9-11

helps to explain some of the steps. The pseudocode representation of this part of the algorithm is given at the right in Figure 9-11.

Some programming languages allow specification of data groups with 200 or more dimensions. In all cases, the number of dimensions that a group has determines the number of subscripts needed to refer to a particular element of the group. Though groups with many dimensions are difficult or impossible for us to visualize, they may be extremely useful in computation. The same kind of program logic—loops within loops—can be used repetitively for all data groups.

The systems designer or programmer who develops an algorithm involving multidimensional data groups should be aware of the programming language that will be

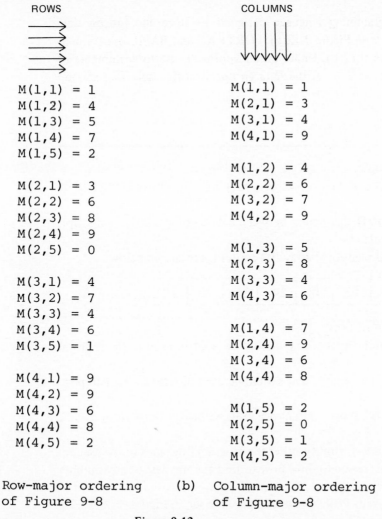

ROWS

COLUMNS

```
M(1,1) = 1          M(1,1) = 1
M(1,2) = 4          M(2,1) = 3
M(1,3) = 5          M(3,1) = 4
M(1,4) = 7          M(4,1) = 9
M(1,5) = 2
                    M(1,2) = 4
M(2,1) = 3          M(2,2) = 6
M(2,2) = 6          M(3,2) = 7
M(2,3) = 8          M(4,2) = 9
M(2,4) = 9
M(2,5) = 0          M(1,3) = 5
                    M(2,3) = 8
M(3,1) = 4          M(3,3) = 4
M(3,2) = 7          M(4,3) = 6
M(3,3) = 4
M(3,4) = 6          M(1,4) = 7
M(3,5) = 1          M(2,4) = 9
                    M(3,4) = 6
                    M(4,4) = 8
M(4,1) = 9
M(4,2) = 9
M(4,3) = 6          M(1,5) = 2
M(4,4) = 8          M(2,5) = 0
M(4,5) = 2          M(3,5) = 1
                    M(4,5) = 2
```

(a) Row-major ordering   (b) Column-major ordering
     of Figure 9-8   of Figure 9-8

Figure 9-12

used to express the algorithm in computer-program form. Some programming languages read, write, and store the data items in a group in **row-major order** (with the first subscript varying *least* rapidly, and the last subscript varying *most* rapidly). Other programming languages read, write, and store the data items in a group in **column-major order** (with the first subscript varying most rapidly, and the last subscript varying least rapidly). The logic within the solution algorithm should be set up to operate similarly.

We assumed row-major ordering in all of the examples in this lesson. That means, for example, that the table in Figure 9-8 was assumed to be ordered as shown in Figure 9-12(a). In contrast, Figure 9-12(b) shows column-major ordering of the table.

PL/I is a common programming language designed to store and process data groups in row-major order as in Figure 9-12(a). FORTRAN and BASIC use column-major ordering as in Figure 9-12(b). Under either approach, the total numbers of elements in the various dimensions of the data groups are often specified as loop controls.

exercises

1. (a) What is a data group?
   (b) Give some examples of data for which grouping capabilities are apt to be appropriate.
2. Using the term COLOR(I), distinguish between a data group name, a subscript, and a subscripted variable.
3. E is an 8-member one-dimensional array. Its contents are shown below.

57	12	03	48	34	16	50	22

   (a) What is the content of E(4)?
   (b) Write the subscripted variable that should be used to refer to the location containing 57.
   (c) Write the subscripted variable that should be used to refer to the Rth position of the array E.
   (d) The variable R, in (c) above, must have a value within the range from _____ to _____ .
4. Refer to Figures 9-2 and 9-3. Modify either the program flowchart or the pseudocode as suggested in this lesson to show how to find the smallest of any number of values.
5. Modify either the program flowchart or the pseudocode in Figures 9-2 and 9-3

to keep track of which position in Vector V contains the smallest value. The position of the smallest value as well as the value itself should be provided as output.

6. The program logic in Figure 9-6 causes a list of four values to be arranged in ascending sequence. To sort these same values into descending sequence, only one processing step must be modified. Identify this step by redrawing that portion of the flowchart in Figure 9-6.

7. The algorithm that you created in response to Exercise 6 should show how to perform a descending sort. Assume the following data items are provided as input to the program that you have planned: 52, .091, 708, 10.
   (a) What output should be provided by the program?
   (b) Perform a procedure execution (including construction of the tables needed) to verify that the program will perform as you intend.
   (c) If the results of your procedure execution in (b) do not match the results you specified in (a), examine both your solution algorithm and your procedure execution to determine where errors have occurred. Make changes needed to eliminate those errors.

8. Refer to Figures 9-6 and 9-7. Modify either the program flowchart or the pseudocode to show how to place in ascending sequence any number of values. An input value of 0 should be recognized as a dummy indicator, signalling that all values to be sorted have been read. When the sort operation is finished, the message SORT COMPLETED should be printed for control purposes.

9. A is a 30-member two-dimensional array with six rows and five columns. S is a simple variable. The contents of these locations have been set to 0; they appear as follows:

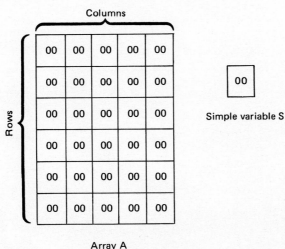

Array A

Show the contents of these locations after the following statements have been executed.

```
10   S = 05
20   A(2,4) = 40
30   A(1,2) = 67
40   A(6,2) = A(4,3) + A(2,4)
50   A(S,1) = 99
60   A(5,4) = A(1,2) - A(2,S-1)
```

10. Construct a program flowchart or use pseudocode to show the logic required in the following problem situation: Read a two-level table SALES into storage. The table has three rows, and each row contains 18 values. Compute the total value of the elements in each row. Provide three computed totals and a grand total, which is the sum of all values, as output. Be sure to plan a well-structured program.

TABLE SEARCHING

In the preceding lesson, we saw that it is sometimes useful to read, process, and write collections of similar data items as a data group rather than as separate data items. We saw how subscript notation can be used to refer to specific elements of a group. We developed solution algorithms to find and print the smallest of a set of values, sort a set of values into ascending sequence, and multiply the elements in a table by list elements in corresponding positions. (In mathematical problem-solving, the last of these algorithms is usually referred to as multiplying a matrix by a vector.)

Tables are very widely used in problem solving. To determine how much sales tax is owed on items purchased at a local supermarket, the checkout clerk often refers to sales tax tables. When preparing annual income tax returns, we refer to other types of tax tables. An insurance representative refers to rating tables to determine the premiums to be charged for insurance policies. Postal clerks refer to tables showing weights and distances to determine mailing costs. The results of market research and statistical analyses are often displayed in tabular form. To convert temperatures from Fahrenheit to Celsius, or English measurements (inches, feet, yards, and so on) to metric units, we use tables. So it should not surprise us that tables are often used in the computer-program representations of solution algorithms.

In programming terminology, reading a table into computer storage is often referred to as **loading a table**. This step usually occurs soon after program execution is initiated, that is to say, in the initialization portion of the program. After a table has been loaded, it can be referred to repetitively during subsequent processing steps. Often another input value that causes a search of the table is read. For example, a payroll application may have as one of its inputs a table showing wage classes and corresponding pay rates. An employee time card submitted as later input may contain the wage class of a particular employee. The class/rate table must

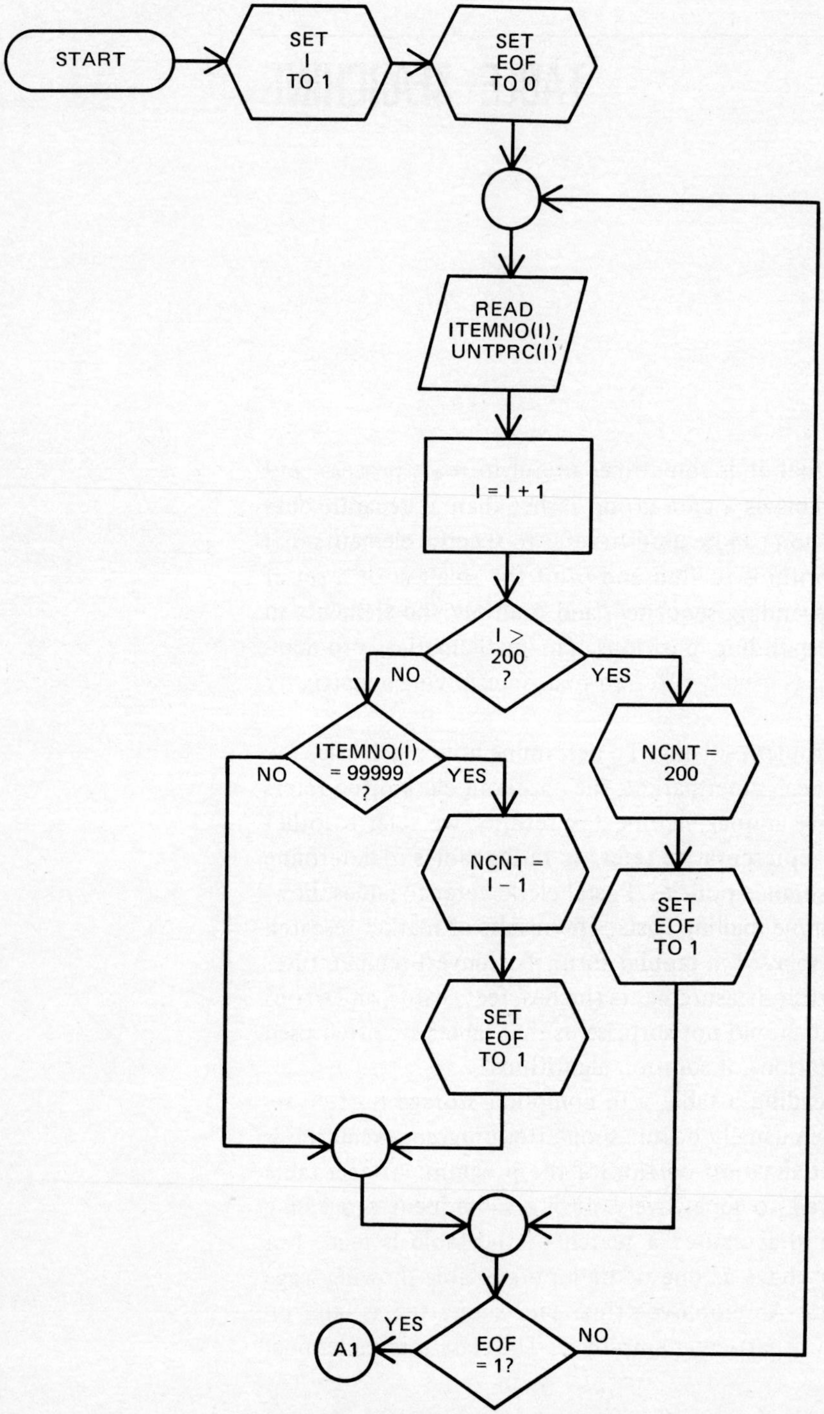

Figure 10-1(a)

be searched to determine what pay rate to use in calculating the employee's pay. This operation is called a **table lookup**.

To understand how tables and table lookups may be applied in practical situations, consider the following example. An algorithm to read a master list of unique item numbers and another master list of corresponding unit prices for registered pharmaceutical products is shown in flowchart form in Figure 10-1(a). The same algorithm appears in pseudocode form in Figure 10-1(b). Each list is a one-dimensional data group. The names ITEMNO and UNTPRC are used for the groups on the program flowchart. Together, the lists of item numbers and unit prices form a table of reference data.

A **DOUNTIL** control structure controls the loading of the table. Two nested **IFTHENELSE** control structures are used because the number of items to be included in the table is not fixed. Therefore, it is not known beforehand exactly how many times the **DOUNTIL** loop needs to be executed during a run.

Since the pharmaceutical products are registered items, the designer of the solution algorithm has determined that not more than 200 items will have to be identified and priced. If less than 200 item numbers are entered, a special input record with an item number of 99999 is to be entered to indicate that the table

```
Start
Set subscript I to 1
Set end-of-file indicator EOF to 0
DOUNTIL no more table entries (EOF=1)
    Read itemno(I), unitprice(I)
    Add 1 to subscript I
    IF I is greater than 200 THEN
        set number of entries NCNT to 200
        set EOF to 1
    ELSE
        IF itemno(I) is equal to 99999 THEN
            set NCNT to I-1
            set EOF to 1
        (ELSE)
        ENDIF
    ENDIF
ENDDO
    .
    .
    .
```

Figure 10-1(b)

(formed by the two lists) is complete. The outermost IFTHENELSE checks the value of the subscript I, which is also used as a count of the number of table entries read into storage. If the maximum number of table entries (200) have been read, a special end-of-file indicator is set to 1. The inner IFTHENELSE checks the item numbers of up to 200 entries to watch for the 99999 input record. If the 99999 record is detected, the special end-of-file indicator is set to 1. Whichever of the tested conditions occurs first causes the DOUNTIL loop to be exited.

Note that, in either case of loop termination, the number of table entries read into storage is placed in NCNT before the end-of-file indicator is set. This value can be used as a loop control when the table is referred to in subsequent processing.

Figure 10-2 shows the processing that occurs after the reference table has been loaded into storage. Here, another type of input is read: inquiries to be processed against the table. Each inquiry consists of an item number and a quantity. A DOWHILE control structure controls the reading of the inquiries.

Because the number of inquiries to be processed will vary from one run of this program to another, a special input containing 99999 as an item number is to be entered as an end-of-input record after all inquiries have been processed. The outermost nested IFTHENELSE checks the item numbers of all inquiries to watch for the 99999 record. When this record is encountered, the ELSE clause (NO path) of the IFTHENELSE is executed. A special *end-of-input (EOI) indicator* is set to 1. This causes the DOWHILE loop controlling the read operations to be exited immediately upon the next test of the EOI indicator value.

For all inputs other than the 99999 record, the THEN clause (YES path) of the outermost IFTHENELSE in Figure 10-2 is executed. This causes a DOWHILE loop to be executed repetitively until either of two conditions exists:

- the item number of the inquiry received as input (called NUMB on the program flowchart) is matched with an item number in the reference table (ITEMNO(I))
- all item numbers in the table have been examined without finding an item number that matches the item number in the inquiry

These conditions are tested for by the nested IFTHENELSE control structures within the DOWHILE. Whichever occurs first causes another indicator—the *out-of-range (OOR) indicator*—to be set to 1. When the OOR indicator is tested and found to be 1, the DOWHILE loop is exited.

When an item number from the item-number portion of the reference table matches the item number of an inquiry (the first condition above), computation occurs before the OOR indicator is set. The unit price corresponding to the item number (from the unit-price portion of the reference table) is multiplied by the quantity entered as input (called QUANT on the flowchart) to determine total

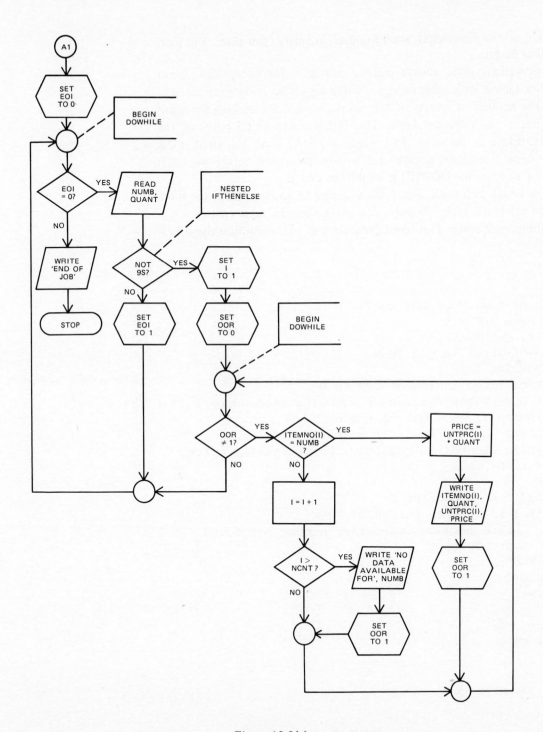

Figure 10-2(a)

cost (called PRICE on the flowchart). Item number, quantity, unit price, and total cost are provided as output.

Table-lookup operations must always include provision for exceptions: input values that do not match with table entries. In this algorithm, whenever the subscript I exceeds the number of entries NCNT, no item number matching the input item number exists in the reference table. The THEN clause (YES path) of the innermost IFTHENELSE is executed. The words NO DATA AVAILABLE FOR followed by the unmatched item number are written as output before the OOR indicator is set to 1 to cause the DOWHILE loop to be exited.

What assumptions have you made about the ordering of entries within the item-number/unit-price reference table? Perhaps you think that the table entries are in ascending item-number sequence. This is not a requirement of the solution algorithm.

```
        .
        .
        .
Set end-of-input indicator EOI to 0
DOWHILE more data (EOI=0)
    Read number, quantity
    IF not end-of-input record THEN
        set subscript I to 1
        set out-of-range indicator OOR to 0
        DOWHILE more table entries or matching item number not found (OOR≠1)
            IF itemno(I) is equal to number THEN
                price = unitprice(I) * quantity
                write itemno(I), quantity, unitprice(I), price
                set OOR to 1
            ELSE
                add 1 to subscript I
                IF I is greater than NCNT THEN
                    write message indicating number not found
                    set OOR to 1
                (ELSE)
                ENDIF
            ENDIF
        ENDDO
    ELSE
        set EOI to 1
    ENDIF
ENDDO
Write end-of-job message
Stop
```

Figure 10-2

The item numbers in the table may be in ascending sequence, or descending sequence, or no particular sequence at all. Because the table-lookup routine starts at the beginning of the table for each inquiry, it will work in any of these cases.

The sequence of entries in a table can affect the efficiency of table searching in terms of processing time, however. Because the table-lookup routine in Figure 10-2 always starts with the first entry and proceeds toward the last, the most-used item number should be the first entry in the table, and the least-used entry should be the last. For example, if 60 percent of the inquiries involve item numbers 55040, 30456, and 32045, these item numbers should be the first ones in the table. The rest of the table should also be sequenced according to frequency of use. The total amount of time required for a run will be determined accordingly.

In cases where (1) the frequency of use of table entries is evenly distributed over the table, (2) the number of entries in the table is very large, or (3) processing efficiency or high system performance is mandatory, a more sophisticated table-lookup routine should be considered. One that is commonly employed is the **binary search**. When this table-lookup technique is used, the entries in the table being searched must be in either ascending or descending sequence according to a particular data item or items that is common to all entries. The portion of an entry that contains that data item or items is called the **key field**. The term *binary* is appropriate for this lookup technique because the portion of the table being searched is halved repeatedly. The search begins with an entry at or near the middle of the table. Based on a comparison, the search continues in either the first half or the second half of the table. The next comparison is near the middle of the half just selected. The search continues by successively halving the portion of the table remaining. Eventually, a match occurs between the **search key** of the data being processed against the table and the key field of a table entry. Alternatively, it is determined that no entry with a matching key field exists in the table. In this case, an exception routine must be carried out.

Look at Figure 10-3(a). This flowchart shows the **main line** of a report-generating program. A flowcharting technique that we have not used before is shown on this flowchart. It is called the **striping convention**. A stripe across the top of a flowcharting symbol indicates that a more detailed description of the function represented by the symbol is provided elsewhere in the set of flowcharts for the system or program being documented. (See the first process symbol in Figure 10-3(a).) Generally, the function represented by the striped symbol is designed such that it can be coded as a separate section of code. It may be implemented as any one of the following program constructs:

- a *routine,* a sequence of instructions that performs one or more specific functions

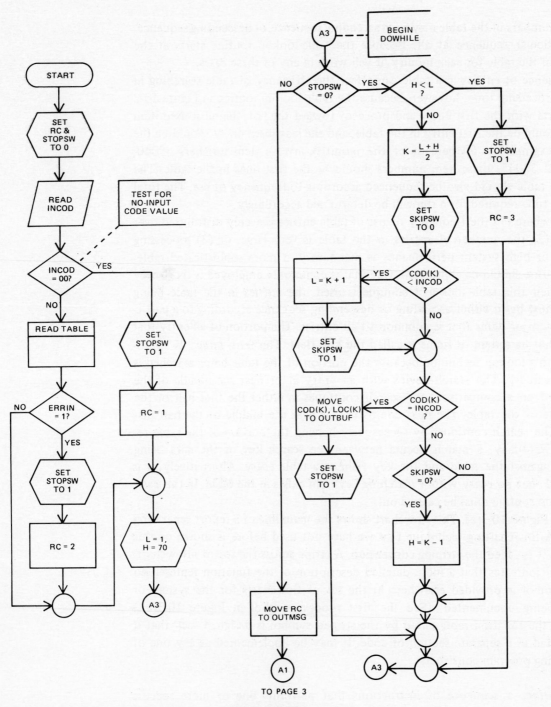

Figure 10-3(a)

```
Start
Set reason code RC to 0
Set stop switch STOPSW to 0
Read office code INCOD
IF INCOD is equal to 00 THEN
    set STOPSW to 1
    RC=1
ELSE
    call read table routine
    IF error indicator ERRIN is equal to 1 THEN
        set STOPSW to 1
        RC=2
    (ELSE)
    ENDIF
ENDIF
Set lower bound L to 1
Set upper bound H to 70
DOWHILE STOPSW is equal to 0
    IF current upper bound H is less than current
      lower bound L THEN
        set STOPSW to 1
        RC=3
    ELSE
        set subscript K equal to (L + H) / 2
        set skip switch SKIPSW to 0
        IF officecode(K) is less than INCOD THEN
            set lower bound L to K + 1
            set SKIPSW to 1
        (ELSE)
        ENDIF
        IF officecode(K) is equal to INCOD THEN
            move officecode(K), officelocation(K) to
              output buffer area
            set STOPSW to 1
        ELSE
            IF SKIPSW is equal to 0 THEN
                set upper bound H to K - 1
            (ELSE)
            ENDIF
        ENDIF
    ENDIF
ENDDO
Move RC to end-of-search message
    .
    .
    .
(additional steps of the report generation algorithm,
which follow the search of the reference table, are
specified here to complete the overall program design)
    .
    .
    .
```

Figure 10-3(b)

- a *subroutine,* usually a generalized sequence of instructions performing a commonly required function, designed and coded in such a way that it can be included in any of numerous routines in a program or system
- a *module*, a logical program unit, designed so that it can be coded, tested, and debugged separately, then included with other modules to form a complete, executable program

We say much more about using a modular approach to system and program development in Lesson 13. For now, you should understand that (1) a program can be designed so that it has functionally identifiable subportions, and (2) the striping convention can be used to show where a particular function occurs in the program flow and to point to the documentation of it.

The striping convention is applied as follows:

1. A horizontal line is drawn within and near the top of the symbol that must be striped.
2. The detailed representation of the function starts and ends with terminal symbols.
3. An identifier is placed above the stripe in the striped symbol, and in the entry terminal symbol of the detailed representation.
4. **A pointer** back to the striped symbol is placed in the exit terminal symbol of the detailed representation.

We can tell from Figure 10-3(a) that a read table function is executed if the test at the first decision-making step (IFTHENELSE control structure) causes the NO path from that step to be followed. The detailed representation of the function is shown on the flowchart in Figure 10-4(a). Note how the flowcharting rules stated above were followed in constructing this flowchart.

If desired, one or more of the symbols on the flowchart in Figure 10-4(a) could be striped. That is, the pointing to flowcharts showing additional details of functions could continue. This approach is sometimes called **modular program flowcharting**.

You may be wondering how a striped symbol differs in meaning from the predefined process symbol, discussed in Lesson 5. A striped symbol always contains the identifier of a portion of the program that is described in greater detail in the same set of flowcharts. The predefined process symbol refers to program logic that is not described in the same set of flowcharts. As the term *predefined* implies, the programmer takes advantage of logic that has already been described elsewhere—for example, in a user's manual or in another set of flowcharts.

Now let's direct our attention to the problem that this algorithm is meant to solve. Assume that 70 company sales offices are identified on a company's internal documents by unique two-digit codes. When reports are printed for external use, however, the sales offices must be identified by location rather than by code number. Each program that provides a report for external use must have access to information associating the office code numbers with the actual office locations. As we noted, Figures 10-3(a) and 10-4(a) show flowcharts of portions of the algorithm. Part (b) of each of these figures shows the same logic in pseudocode form. We need only be concerned with these portions of the algorithm at this time.

Execution begins at the first step in the main line of the program (Figure 10-3). A storage area set aside for a *reason code* (RC) is initialized to 0. At the end of program execution, the content of this area will be printed as part of the output to indicate what happened during execution of the program. If a reason code value of 0 is printed, the program can be assumed to have executed to completion successfully; any other reason code indicates that a problem was encountered.

A second storage area, used for a *stop switch* (STOPSW), is also set to 0. This stop switch is a specific example of how another important programming technique—the use of **program switches**—can be applied. In general, a program switch is used to set up the logic needed to deal with a special condition that may arise during processing. It may be implemented in any of several ways, depending on the hardware and software characteristics of the computer system in use. In this case, the switch is simply a particular storage location or group of storage locations that contains either all 1 bits or all 0 bits. When the location contains 1 bits, the switch is *ON*; when the location contains 0 bits, the switch is *OFF*. The switch is set to 0 (OFF) in the first preparation step in Figure 10-3. As we shall see, it is tested, and it is set to 1 (ON) if appropriate, in succeeding steps in the program.

In the next processing step, an office code (INCOD) is read as input. A check is made to determine whether or not the office code is 00, a special no-input code value indicating that no specific office code was specified for this processing run. If the office code is 00, both the reason code and the stop switch are set to 1; that is, the operations on the YES path from the first decision-making step are carried out. Execution of the program continues, but we know that no association of office code to office location has to be made during this particular run.

If the office code is not 00, the read table routine flowcharted in detail in Figure 10-4(a) is executed. A variable K to be used as a subscript and an error indicator (ERRIN) are set to 0. Another program switch, in this case a *first-time switch* (FTSW), is set to 1. A DOUNTIL control structure is used to control the reading of the two-digit office codes for the company's 70 sales offices and the corresponding office locations into storage as two one-dimensional arrays (COD and LOC). Together, the arrays form a reference table.

Because the office-code/office-location reference table is to be accessed using a binary search technique, the entries in the table must be ordered. A sequence check is performed to make certain that they are. This is where the first-time switch

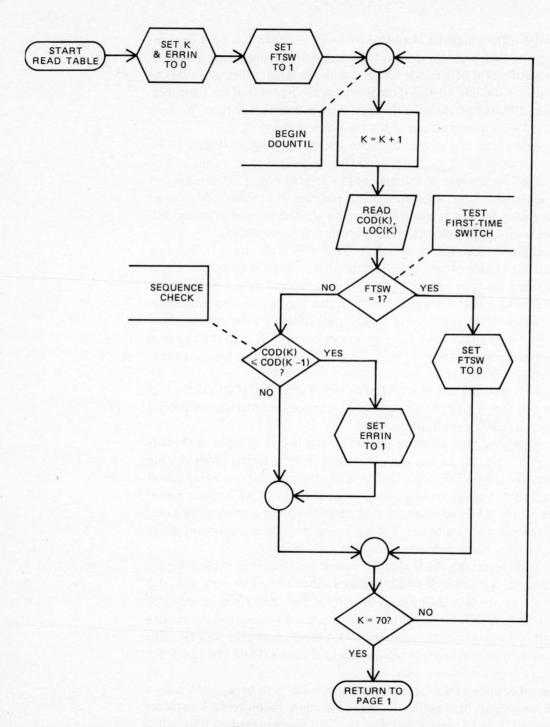

Figure 10-4(a)

is used. To avoid sequence checking the first code number against a preceding code number (because there is no code number preceding the first one), FTSW is initially set to 1. This causes the YES path (THEN clause of the first nested IFTHENELSE) to be executed the first time it is tested. Then the first-time switch is set to 0, or OFF; it remains OFF for the rest of the program. The YES path of this decision-making step is not taken again (because all succeeding code numbers must be sequence checked).

Each office code number must be greater than the one that precedes it. If it is not, the error indicator (ERRIN) is set to 1. The value of the error indicator should be checked by any routine that causes this read table routine to be executed, before the reference table that it loads into storage is used in subsequent processing.

The DOUNTIL loop in Figure 10-4 is exited when all 70 table entries have been read into storage. Control is then returned to the main line of the program.

In the next processing step (see Figure 10-3), the value of the error indicator is checked. If it is 1, indicating a sequence error, the stop switch is set to 1 (thus insuring that a certain DOWHILE pattern later in the program will not be executed). The reason code is set to 2. It will be printed later to tell output recipients that a sequence error was detected when loading the reference table. Since something is wrong with the table, it is pointless to use it until the errors have been identified and eliminated.

If the error indicator is not equal to 1, the reference table is assumed to be correct and available in storage. A variable L, used to store the *lower bound* of the reference

```
Start
Set subscript K to 0
Set error indicator ERRIN to 0
Set first-time switch FTSW to 1
DOUNTIL all table entries read (K = 70)
   Add 1 to subscript K (K = K + 1)
   Read officecode(K), officelocation(K)
   IF FTSW is equal to 1 THEN
      set FTSW to 0
   ELSE
      IF officecode(K) is less than or equal to officecode(K-1) THEN
         set ERRIN to 1
      (ELSE)
      ENDIF
   ENDIF
ENDDO
Return to caller
```

Figure 10-4(b)

table, is set to 1. A variable H, used to store the *upper bound* of the table, is set to 70 (because there are 70 entries). Then a DOWHILE loop is entered the first time. If the stop switch is not equal to 0, the DOWHILE loop is exited immediately, because either INCOD contains the special no-input code value 00 or the reference table is bad. In either case, the reference table should not be used in processing.

If the stop switch is equal to 0, the processing steps within the DOWHILE loop are carried out. In this loop, a binary search of the reference table is performed. First, the current upper bound H of the table is compared against the current lower bound L to determine if L is greater. The first time, the answer is obvious, but the values of H and L will change, as we shall see. This time the NO path (ELSE clause) of the first nested IFTHENELSE within the DOWHILE is executed.

The *midpoint* of the office-code/office-location reference table is computed by adding the lower bound L and the upper bound H, and then dividing their sum by 2. The result of the division operation is stored in the variable K, which is used as a subscript during table processing. A *skip switch* (SKIPSW) is set to 0. It will be used later to control whether the upper bound or lower bound of the table is changed.

Next, the current value of INCOD (the office code number read as input) is compared to the midpoint value of the code-number portion of the reference table— COD(K). (K = (1 + 70)/2 the first time through—on most systems, this result would be truncated to 35.)

The program then proceeds as follows:

- If the value of COD(K) is less than the value of INCOD, the upper half of the reference table is searched.
- If the value of COD(K) is equal to the value of INCOD, the table search is ended because the code numbers match.
- If neither of these conditions is true, COD(K) is greater than INCOD, so the lower half of the reference table is searched.

These tests are set up in a structured manner as IFTHENELSE patterns. The skip switch controls whether the lower bound or the upper bound of the table is changed if the search must be continued further.

If COD(K) is not equal to INCOD, the DOWHILE loop is executed again. The value of INCOD is tested against the midpoint value of the half of the table that contains the code number, as indicated by previous algorithmic steps. As before, if the compared values are equal, the search is ended. If not, the skip switch indicates in which half of the divided table (that is, in which quarter of the table) the code number can be found. Halving continues in this manner until the search is successful, or until it is proved that the code number is not at the point where it should be in the reference table. In the former case, the code number and the corresponding

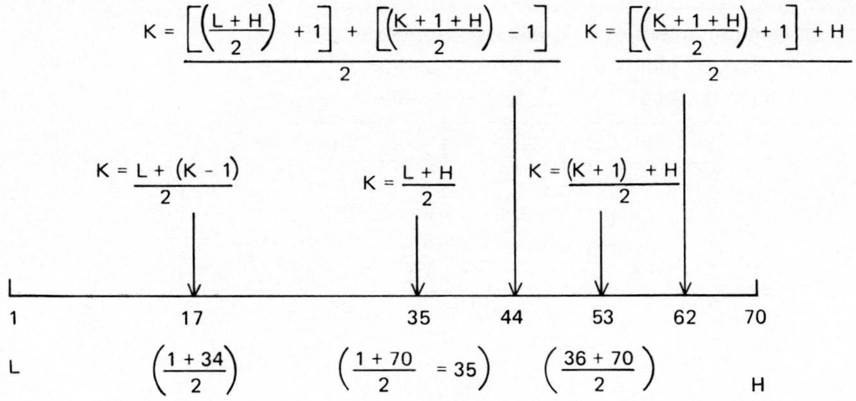

$$K = \frac{\left[\left(\frac{L+H}{2}\right) + 1\right] + \left[\left(\frac{K+1+H}{2}\right) - 1\right]}{2} \qquad K = \frac{\left[\left(\frac{K+1+H}{2}\right) + 1\right] + H}{2}$$

$$K = \frac{L + (K-1)}{2} \qquad K = \frac{L+H}{2} \qquad K = \frac{(K+1) + H}{2}$$

| 1 | 17 | 35 | 44 | 53 | 62 | 70 |

L $\qquad \left(\frac{1+34}{2}\right) \qquad \left(\frac{1+70}{2} = 35\right) \qquad \left(\frac{36+70}{2}\right) \qquad$ H

Figure 10-5

office location are moved into an output buffer area for subsequent printing as part of the output report. In the latter case, which is recognized when adjustments to the original lower and upper bounds of the table cause them to coincide or overlap, the reason code is set to 3 and the stop switch is set to 1. This causes the DOWHILE loop to be exited when the value of the stop switch is tested again at the beginning of the loop.

The halving or "zeroing in" procedure accomplished by the binary search technique is illustrated schematically in Figure 10-5. As in the program flowchart, H represents the upper bound, or highest value, in the table; L represents the lower bound, or lowest value; and K is the computed value used as a subscript to adjust the bounds of the table search area as the search progresses.

As mentioned earlier, binary search methods are particularly valuable when a table contains a large number of entries. In a table with 1000 entries, a binary search reduces the maximum number of comparisons from 1000 to 10. The probability of finding a match doubles each time the table is halved. In mathematical terms, the number of comparisons required to do a binary search of n items is less than $\log_2 T(n)$ where $T(n)$ is the next larger power of 2 greater than or equal to n. To do a linear search of n items requires an average of $n/2$ comparisons. This difference in performance is highlighted by the table in Figure 10-6.

Binary search methods should also be considered when a large number of inquiries must be processed against a table during a typical processing run. The algorithm in Figure 10-3 explains how to search the reference table to find a match to one office code number received as input. With slight modification, it could be structured to process not just one but a variable number of office codes. The read table routine in Figure 10-4 would not have to be changed. And it should not be executed more than once. Some modifications to the program logic in Figure 10-3 would be required (see Exercise 12).

Number of table entries to be searched	Maximum number of compares by binary search method	Average number of compares by linear search method
2	1	1
2–4	2	1–2
4–8	3	2–4
8–16	4	4–8
16–32	5	8–16
32–64	6	16–32
.	.	.
.	.	.
.	.	.
512–1024	10	256–512
.	.	.
.	.	.
.	.	.

Figure 10-6

This example also shows how helpful program switches can be in handling certain conditions that may arise during processing. We saw here a stop switch, first-time switch, and skip switch. In a sense, the error indicator is also a program switch. But program switches must be used with care. Otherwise programming errors, such as forgetting to initialize a switch to a particular value, or forgetting to reset it later, are almost certain to occur.

The use of routines, subroutines, and modules is often key to the successful development of a solution algorithm. We saw in this lesson how a read table routine can be set up and referenced from the main line of a program. As noted earlier, Lesson 13 treats the modular approach to system and program development in greater detail.

exercises

1. (a) What is a table-lookup operation?
   (b) Give some examples (other than those given in this book) of common situations where table-lookup operations are used in problem solving.
2. The table-lookup routine in Figure 10-2 is effective, but it is not particularly efficient. The routine always begins searching for a new item number at the beginning of the table. Modify the solution algorithm in Figures 10-1 and 10-2 as follows: Assume that the input used to construct the table and the input referring to the table are to be processed in item-number sequence. Include sequence checks in the solution algorithm for verification. Terminate execution

if (a) an item number equal to or lower than the preceding item number is provided as table input, or (b) an item number lower than the preceding item number is provided as input referring to the table. Begin each table search at the point in the item-number portion of the table where the preceding item number was found. You may express the revised solution algorithm in either flowchart or pseudocode form. Be sure to plan a well-structured program.

3. (a) Distinguish between a routine, a subroutine, and a module.
   (b) Describe a specific problem situation where use of a routine is apt to be appropriate in setting up the problem-solving logic required.
   (c) Repeat (b) above, but for a subroutine.
   (d) Repeat (b) above, but for a module.

4. (a) What is the striping convention?
   (b) Explain how striping is employed on a program flowchart.
   (c) Distinguish between the striping convention and modular program flowcharting.

5. Explain how a binary search technique can be applied in searching a table of U.S. cities and their populations to find the population of the city CHICAGO.

6. For what kinds of problem situations is use of a binary search apt to be especially appropriate?

Refer to Figures 10-3 and 10-4 to complete Exercises 7 through 11.

7. What search key is used in this solution algorithm?

8. What is the key field of a reference table entry?

9. (a) Identify three program switches used in this solution algorithm.
   (b) Explain how each of the three switches that you named is used.

10. (a) What is the purpose of the reason code that is used in this algorithm?
    (b) List and explain the values that the reason code may be assigned.

11. (a) Assume that the value 6 is submitted as input and assigned to INCOD. What is the relative position in the table of the first table value compared to INCOD?
    (b) What is the position in the table of the second table value compared to INCOD?
    (c) Assume that office code number 6 occupies the sixth relative position in the code-number portion of the reference table. How many times will the DOWHILE loop be executed before the matching code number is found?

12. Modify the portion of the solution algorithm shown in Figure 10-3 to provide for the processing of a variable number of office codes received as input. You may assume that one input is fully processed (and the corresponding office location printed on an output report) before another office code is read as input.

13. Use program flowcharting or pseudocode to plan a well-structured program that reads N and an N-member single-level table T. Include checks to make certain that the members of A are unique and in ascending order. Program execution should terminate if they are not. If they are, in subsequent processing steps, the program should read ARG, an input value to be processed against the table.

- If ARG is less than A(1), set CODE equal to 0. Print out ARG, A(1), and CODE.
- If ARG is equal to some member of A, set CODE equal to 1. Print out ARG and CODE.
- If ARG is between A(1) and A(N), but there is no member of A equal to ARG, set CODE equal to 2. Print out ARG, CODE, and the member of A that is closest to but not greater than ARG.
- If ARG is greater than A(N), set CODE equal to 3. Print out ARG, A(N), and CODE.

14. Repeat Exercise 13 but allow for a variable number of inputs to be processed against the table. An input value of 999 for ARG should be recognized as an end-of-file indicator. The program should print an end-of-job message as verification that all input has been processed.

PROCESSING SEQUENTIAL FILES

The programmer directs a great deal of attention to the logic within a program, but he or she must also be conscious of the *environment* in which the program will operate. If the execution of a program is initiated by a user at a terminal, to meet the user's problem-solving needs, the program is said to operate in an **online-processing environment**. Such a program is often an independent entity; it generates its own input or accepts input directly from the user, without that input being operated on beforehand by another program. It provides output that is routed directly to the user or others; the output is not used as input to another program. Any program designed to solve one specific problem is apt to operate in this fashion. For example, a single program may plot the path of an object fired vertically from the earth's surface as a function of time, according to a ballistics formula. Another single program may determine when return on investment will begin in a business venture, given principal, rate of interest to be compounded annually, and an accumulated sum to be attained. In effect, such a program is a system in itself.

In a typical business organization, many computer programs are run on a regularly scheduled basis. Large volumes of input are collected and processed as sets, or **batches**, by the first of a series of interrelated programs, during a single processing run. Each complete series of programs is designed to meet the data-processing requirements of one organizational function—payroll, accounts receivable, billing, or inventory control, for example. The complete series of programs forms a system. Source documents within the system may be used to create inputs for one or more programs, and outputs generated by one program may serve as inputs for one or more other programs. The programs are said to operate in a **batch-processing environment**.

Whether a system comprises one program or several programs, it can be described by a system flowchart. The simplest type of system flowchart was introduced in Lesson 2 of this book. It represents one computer program, which accepts one form of input, and provides one form of output. The system flowchart that we discussed in Lesson 2 is shown again in Figure 11-1. An alternative system flowchart for the same system is shown in Figure 11-2. As Figure 11-2 indicates, basic input/output symbols can be replaced with specialized input/output symbols on system flowcharts.

The **document symbol** (▱) is the most frequently used specialized symbol for input/output media. It represents data in the form of hard-copy input or output of any type. For example, it may represent printed output from a high-speed printer, optical marks on cards to be read by an optical character recognition (OCR) device, or a printed listing produced at a terminal.

The **punched-card symbol** (▱) represents data on a punched card of any style and size. Any applicable data-representation code may be used, provided that the data is actually punched on the card. (If data is simply *printed* on a card, the document symbol should be used instead of the punched-card symbol.)

Thus, without any additional wording, the system flowchart in Figure 11-2 indicates that input to the monthly billing program is in the form of punched cards and that output is in the form of a printed document. Such information is valuable to persons examining a system flowchart.

Figure 11-3 shows a system flowchart for a system that performs master-file updating at a large publishing company. As we learned in Lesson 5, a master file is a collection of related records containing relatively permanent data essential to system processing. Even permanent data must be changed occasionally, however, and updating of master files for one or more systems is required at almost all data-processing installations. Updating a master file is called **file maintenance,** and execution of a program that performs file maintenance is referred to as a **file maintenance run.**

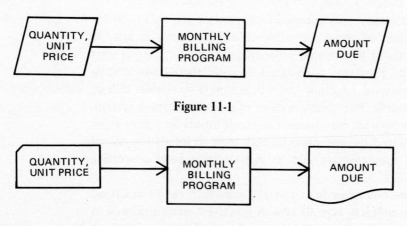

Figure 11-1

Figure 11-2

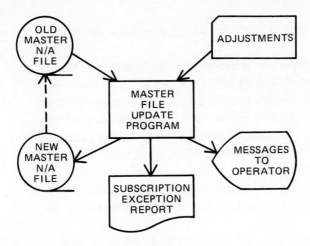

Figure 11-3

The publishing company using the system described in Figure 11-3 stores the names and addresses of all its magazine subscribers in a master name and address file (master N/A file). The file is processed weekly to perform such operations as:

- Add names and addresses of new subscribers
- Delete names and addresses of subscribers for whom all subscriptions have expired
- Identify subscribers whose subscriptions will expire within two issues, so that warning notices can be mailed to them
- Modify records of current subscribers who have subscribed to additional publications, renewed subscriptions, or allowed one or more, but not all, of their subscriptions to expire.

This system flowchart indicates that master-file updating is performed by a master file update program. There are two inputs to the program. One is the current master N/A file, called the old master N/A file to distinguish it from the new master N/A file, which will be created by the program. The **magnetic-tape symbol** ($\bigcirc$) indicates that this file is stored on magnetic tape. The second input is a deck of punched cards showing adjustments to be made to the master N/A file. This file is the transaction, or detail, file.

The master file update program provides three forms of output. One is an updated (or new) master N/A file, which will be used as the current (or old) master file the next time that this program is executed. Programmers often use broken lines as shown in Figure 11-3 to indicate a "turnaround file." The new master N/A file may also be used by other programs (for example, by a print program that prepares address labels for use in mailing).

A second output is an exception report of subscriptions that will expire within the next two issues. This output is provided as a printed document.

A third output is represented by the **display symbol** ($\bigcirc$). This symbol can be used to represent any kind of transitory data not in hard-copy form—cathode-ray tube (CRT) displays, computer-system console displays, and the like. It may also represent intermediate output data used for control during processing, such as is commonly provided to the computer operator or a terminal user. In Figure 11-3, the output represented by the display symbol consists of messages describing error conditions that occur during processing, providing instructions to the operator, and signalling end of job.

A major consideration when processing records from a file on magnetic tape or punched cards is that the records must be accessed in the order in which they are stored on the tape or cards. It would take far too long to spin a tape backward or forward looking for a particular record. There is no facility for re-reading the fifth card prior to the current card from the card reader, for example, or to skip six cards, read a card, and then go back to read the skipped cards. Instead, a particular record can be accessed only after all preceding records on the file have been accessed. We say that **sequential processing** of the records is required.

So that sequential processing can be performed in an efficient, effective manner, the records in a magnetic-tape or punched-card master file are arranged in sequence according to a particular data item or items common to all records in the file. The portion of the record that contains the data is called the **control field**. For example, the control field of records in a master payroll file may contain employee number, the control field of records in a master inventory file may contain part number, and so on. All records to be included in the file must have the required control field, and the field must contain valid data.

An additional requirement of sequential processing is that any transaction records to be processed against a sequential master file must be in the same sequence as the master file records. During program execution, the control field value of a transaction record is compared with the control field values of successive master records until an equal comparison or match results. If transaction records and master records were not arranged in the same sequence before the comparisons were made, some master file records would be read long before their matching transaction records were accessed. It is likely that few if any matches would occur.

For these reasons, a sequential master file update program is seldom an independent entity; it is not a system in itself. The system flowchart in Figure 11-4 shows the four steps usually involved in even the most basic system for updating a sequential magnetic-tape master file.

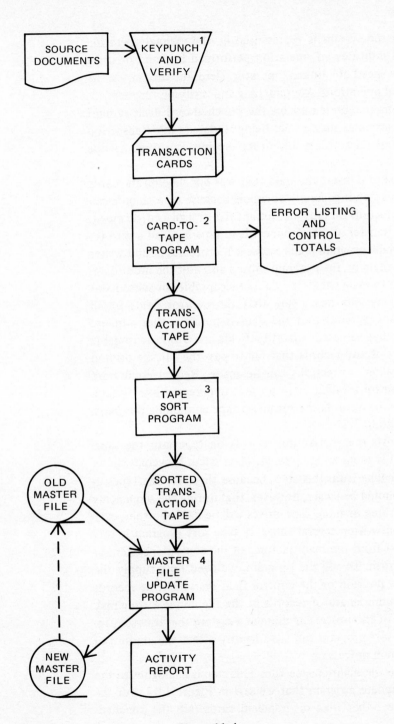

Figure 11-4

The first processing step in the system is represented by the **manual operation symbol** (⬡). This symbol indicates an operation performed by hand or using equipment that operates at the speed of a human operator. Here, the text inside the symbol tells us that two manual operations—keypunching and verifying—are needed. The output of these operations is represented by the **punched-card deck symbol** (▱). Depending on the particular master file being updated, the transaction cards in this deck may represent sales orders, inventory receipts, customer credits or debits, and so on.

The second processing step is to convert the data that was punched on the cards into data on magnetic tape. This step is generally advisable because tape records can be processed faster than cards, records on tape are not apt to be misplaced, dropped, or disarranged, and so on. The transfer of data from cards to tape is called a **card-to-tape run**. The simplest **card-to-tape program** reads each card, processes it, and writes a corresponding tape record. Generally, the program should also **edit** the input data, that is, it should perform tests to insure that the data is acceptable for subsequent processing. Typical editing operations make sure that the control fields of all records contain data and (if appropriate) that the data is numeric, that numeric fields do not contain blanks, that values in quantity fields are within reasonable limits, and so on. The contents of any records that fail to pass the edit are printed as an **error listing** so that required corrections can be made. Record counts are accumulated and printed as **control totals** to help prevent undetected loss of data. A second output of the card-to-tape run is the magnetic tape containing the transaction records processed successfully.

The third processing step **sorts** the transaction records on tape into the same sequence as the master file that is going to be updated. The system flowchart shows one input tape and one output tape from this step, because these are the tapes in which we are interested. You should be aware, however, that during the sequencing (sorting) operations, tapes on three or more tape drives will be used. Further, each of these tapes will be read and written several times. A **tape sort program** is very complex. Usually, it is obtained from the manufacturer of the computer system or from a software development firm. To use the program, we need only supply the sort specifications—such as the position of the control field on which the records are to be sorted and the maximum length of records in the file. Since sorting may account for a large percentage of the processing done in a system that uses sequential files, the efficiency of the sort program can significantly affect the amount of computer time required for system processing.

Finally, the fourth step is the file maintenance run. This step is analogous to the execution of the master file update program that we saw in Figure 11-3, but the transaction records are on tape rather than on punched cards (see the punched-card symbol containing "Adjustments" in Figure 11-3). One output of the program is the new master file, which will be used as the old master file the next time this program is run. Another is a printed **activity report**, indicating which master file records were actually updated. Additional outputs may be created, depending on the particular type of application being processed. For example, the update run of an accounts receivable system may provide a listing of the account numbers and balances for all customers whose accounts have exceeded specified credit limits as a result of the update run.

Remember that each program represented by one process symbol on a system flowchart must be described in detail on a program flowchart. Let's direct our attention now to the processing steps *within* a program that performs sequential file maintenance. Any of several programming techniques can be used to match transaction records with corresponding master records for updating. One approach is shown in flowchart form in Figure 11-5 and in pseudocode form in Figure 11-6.

Two assumptions are basic to the successful execution of the program outlined in this design documentation:

1. The master file and the transaction file are in the same sequence according to the control fields M and T, respectively.
2. There is at least one data record in each of the files.

All such assumptions made during the design stage of program development must be recognized and verified before the design plan is accepted. They should be stated clearly in the program documentation and pointed out whenever changes to the program or its inputs are discussed.

As Figures 11-5 and 11-6 indicate, planning for end-of-file processing is an important part of sequential file updating. In this program, three storage locations are used as program switches. These switches are set to either 0 or 1 in processing steps represented by the preparation symbols on the program flowchart. They are tested at some of the decision-making steps, and subsequent processing steps are determined accordingly. The switches are:

- EOFT (*end-of-file transaction*): if set to 0, a new transaction record is read; if set to 1, the end of the transaction file has been encountered.
- EOFM (*end-of-file master*): if set to 0, a new master record is read; if set to 1, the end of the master file has been encountered.
- EOFB (*end-of-file both*): if set to 0, the DOUNTIL loop is re-executed because one or more records remains to be processed; if set to 1, the DOUNTIL loop is exited, because end-of-file records on both the master file and the detail file have been encountered, so processing can be terminated.

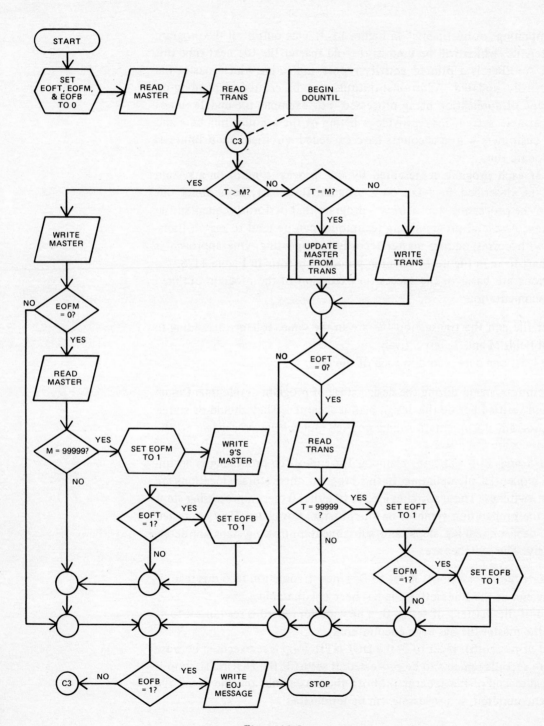

Figure 11-5

```
Start
Set end-of-file switches to 0
Read master record
Read transaction record
DOUNTIL both master and transaction
  at end-of-file (EOFB = 1)
    IF transaction greater than master THEN
       write master record
       IF more master records (EOFM = 0) THEN
          read master record
          IF end-of-file master record THEN
             set EOFM to 1
             write end-of-file (9s) record
             IF end-of-file transaction record already processed (EOFT=1) THEN
                set EOFB to 1
             (ELSE)
             ENDIF
          (ELSE)
          ENDIF
       (ELSE)
       ENDIF
    ELSE
       IF transaction equals master THEN
          update master from transaction
       ELSE
          write transaction record
       ENDIF
       IF more transaction records (EOFT = 0) THEN
          read transaction record
          IF end-of-file transaction record THEN
             set EOFT to 1
             IF end-of-file master record already processed (EOFM=1) THEN
                set EOFB to 1
             (ELSE)
             ENDIF
          (ELSE)
          ENDIF
       (ELSE)
       ENDIF
    ENDIF
ENDDO
Write end-of-job message
Stop
```

Figure 11-6

The overall reading of transaction and master records in this well-structured program is controlled by means of a DOUNTIL control structure. Subsequent compare operations are set up as nested IFTHENELSE control structures. Unmatched master records are written out unchanged to the new master file. Unmatched transaction records are noted on a printed report for subsequent examination by the persons responsible for providing input to the run. Either an error has occurred in the preparation of input or a new addition is to be made to the master file. In any case, a new addition need not be made at this time. This approach helps to prevent additions of invalid data to the master file.

When matching transaction and master records are processed, the master file is updated. A predefined process symbol appears on this path of the flowchart. In this case, we can assume that the master file updating operations are described in pseudocode form or on another program flowchart.

You should go over both the flowchart in Figure 11-5 and the pseudocode in Figure 11-6 to insure that you understand fully the program logic within this solution algorithm. Because it shows one approach to sequential file maintenance in a basic form, it may be useful as a model when you are confronted with the task of planning a sequential master file update program.

SAMPLE PROBLEM 11.1

Problem: All shipments of sporting goods from Beech Manufacturing, Inc., are generated in response to sales orders prepared by sales personnel at field locations. These sales orders serve as source documents for an inventory, order-writing, and invoicing system that accesses data in two master files stored on magnetic tape: a master inventory file, and a master customer file. The system creates a priced transaction file on magnetic tape for subsequent use in a system that performs various types of sales analyses. It prepares and prints a combined invoice and shipping-order form that is routed to the shipping department and also generates input for the company's accounts-receivable system.

It is expected that several computer programs will be required in this system. Intermediate files (also called temporary or scratch files) may be created as necessary. Hard-copy reports should be provided to show sales orders that cannot be processed successfully by the system until certain corrections are made to them, actioned items in inventory, and any unusual sales conditions warranting the attention of accounting-department personnel (for example, customers for whom no master customer records exist or whose credit limits have been exceeded as a result of preceding order-writing and billing activities).

Solution: The system flowchart for this inventory, order-writing, and invoicing application is shown in Figure 11-7. It represents six processing steps during which a combined invoice and shipping-order is printed for each sales order received as input. The steps are summarized below.

First, the sales orders serve as source documents to a processing step performed manually. Item cards are keypunched and then verified, either through the use of a verifier or by visual examination.

Next, the data that was punched on the cards is transferred to magnetic tape during a card-to-tape run. The major output of this run is that magnetic tape, called the current item file, which contains the item records intended for subsequent processing. The contents of any cards that cannot be processed successfully are printed on an input exception report.

Before the records in the current item file can be processed against the records in the master inventory file, which contains records in item-number sequence, they must be sorted into item-number sequence. Step 3 accomplishes this sorting. Note the use of the annotation symbol to provide additional explanation—the master file control fields—on this system flowchart. We saw this symbol earlier on program flowcharts. It can appear on both types of flowcharts.

Step 4 of this system accomplishes two functions. First, cost data is added to each record in the sorted item file (transaction file) so that it can be used to print line items on the invoice and shipping-order form. Second, the master inventory file is updated. Master-record fields that may be affected are the on-hand field (reduced by the number of items shipped) and the back-ordered field (increased by the number of items ordered when an insufficient quantity of the item is present in inventory). Three outputs are provided by the price and update program that controls these functions: the priced transaction file, the new master inventory file, and a printed activity report showing all actioned items.

In step 5, the priced transaction file is sorted. The records must be rearranged into customer-number sequence before they can be processed against the master customer file.

The inputs to the processing run of step 6 are the sorted priced transaction file and the master customer file. The outputs are the invoice and shipping-order form, the updated master customer file, and a sales exception report showing factors needing accounting-department attention. After the heading for the shipping-order form is printed from the data in the master customer record, the line items are printed from the data in the priced transaction file. The invoice total is calculated, printed on the invoice and shipping-order form, and applied to update the customer's accounts-receivable data on the master customer file.

At the end of these six steps, the invoice and shipping-order form is printed. The new master inventory file, the new master customer file, and the priced transaction

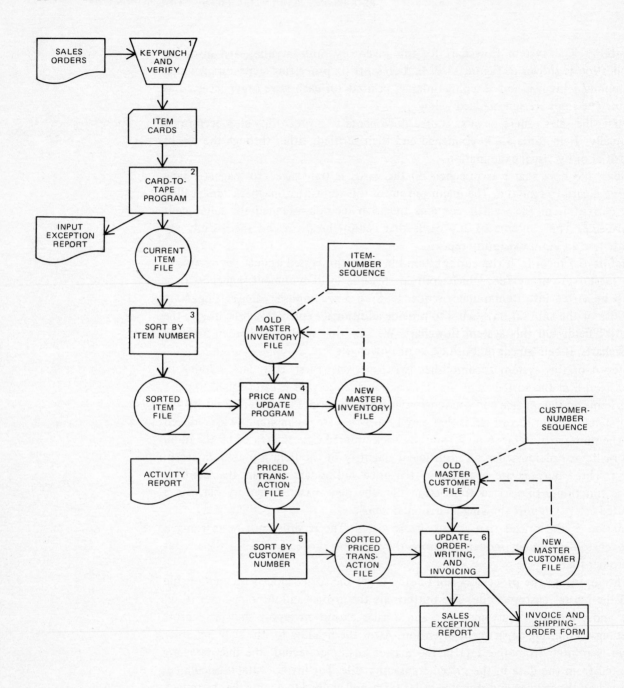

Figure 11-7

file are ready for subsequent processing. For example, the master inventory file can be processed to prepare an inventory management report. The master customer file can be used to prepare an aged accounts-receivable report. The priced transaction file contains sales data needed for sales analyses and summary reporting.

exercises

1. Define the following terms:
   (a) online-processing environment
   (b) batch-processing environment
   (c) file maintenance run
   (d) card-to-tape run
2. What is the most significant characteristic of a magnetic-tape file, insofar as determining how records in the file must be processed?
3. Explain, in general terms, why sorting is often required in a business data processing system.
4. (a) List the program switches used in the solution algorithm in Figures 11-5 and 11-6.
   (b) Explain the processing steps in which each switch is used.
5. Refer to the solution algorithm in Figures 11-5 and 11-6. Suppose we cannot assume there will be at least one data record in each input file. Modify either the flowchart or the pseudocode representation of the algorithm to show what modifications to the program logic would be required.
6. Modify the solution algorithm in Figure 11-5 or 11-6 to use a count of the number of master records processed as a control total for a program run. The count should be: (1) initialized to 0, (2) increased by 1 whenever a master record is written as output, (3) compared to an existing count in the 9s master record provided as input, with a warning message printed if the accumulated count and the count in the 9s record do not match, and (4) written in the new 9s record for use as a control total during the next program run.
7. Refer to Figure 11-7 and the text description of the system to answer the following questions:
   (a) What are some editing operations that may be performed in step 2?
   (b) Why is step 3 necessary?
   (c) What happens in step 4?
   (d) What files in the system are used as turnaround files?
   (e) What hard-copy reports are provided as output of the system?
   (f) Who might use each of the reports that you named in response to 7(e)? How?
8. A large hotel pays for data-processing services offered by a local service bureau. It provides punched-card employee time cards as input and relies on the center to

perform its weekly payroll processing. Each input card (or record) contains an employee number and the number of hours that the employee worked during a day of the previous week. From one to five cards may be submitted for each employee. First, the cards must be transcribed from cards to tape, so that data handling is easier and minimum computer time is required for subsequent processing. Then the records on tape must be placed in ascending sequence by employee number. Finally, the total hours worked by each employee are to be accumulated, printed with employee number on a weekly payroll report, and written with employee number to a magnetic-tape weekly payroll file for subsequent processing. Construct a system flowchart for this weekly payroll system. Be sure to include provisions to insure that qualitative data processing is performed.

9. The system flowchart that you constructed in response to Exercise 8 should include three programs. The third of these performs the accumulation and printing described above. Draw a program flowchart for that program. In doing so, provide for the following:

(a) Sequence checking of all input records, to be sure that records are in ascending employee-number order and to recognize when all cards for an employee have been processed.

(b) Use of a program switch to avoid sequence checking of the first input record, since there is no previous employee number to which the employee number in this record can be compared.

(c) Storing employee number as it changes for use in comparing against a subsequent employee number.

(d) Calling an error routine (described in detail on another flowchart created as part of the documentation for this system) if a sequence error occurs, and then terminating the program.

(e) Computing total hours worked for each employee.

(f) Providing the required outputs.

(g) Recognizing a record containing 9s in its six-digit employee number field as an end-of-file indicator.

Assume that at least one data record other than the end-of-file record will be processed during a run. Be sure to print and write totals for the last employee for whom data is entered, as well as for each other employee. Your plan should show how to construct a well-structured program for this application.

RANDOM-ACCESS PROCESSING

In recent years, and at an ever-increasing pace, data-processing operations have been greatly enhanced by the development of **data-communication** facilities. These facilities make it possible to process data at a point remote from the point of data origin. Under **remote job entry (RJE)**, both data and programs to process that data are entered into a computer system from a source geographically distant from the central computer installation where the data processing occurs.

An **offline system** accepts input by means of a device not under direct control of the major computer (for subsequent forwarding as computer input). For example, data may be recorded on paper tape, converted to signals suitable for transmission over a communications network, then reconverted to paper-tape form by a device at the central computer installation for subsequent batched input to the computer.

An **online system** receives data and programs directly into the computer and transmits data directly from the computer to where it is used, without intermediate transcription. For example, data entered at shop-floor terminals in a large production facility may be routed to a central computer and accepted as direct input immediately to be applied against one or more company master files.

A **realtime system** uses online capabilities to accept input and provide output so quickly that the output can be useful in controlling a current "live" activity. Airlines reservation systems, credit authorization systems established at retail department stores, and the complex tracking systems used to control manned space flights are examples of realtime applications.

The basic components of one type of data-processing/data-communication system, an inquiry application, are shown in Figure 12-1. Processing within this system is initiated by a user at a terminal who wants to know the current status of an item in inventory. He or she enters an inquiry that initiates execution of the program to determine stock status. This program searches the master stock file and provides the requested information to the user, who can then take appropriate action.

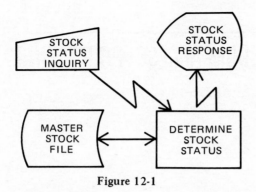

Figure 12-1

The file-reference capabilities essential to successful execution of the system in Figure 12-1 are possible because of techniques for **random-access processing**. When these capabilities are available, a record can be written into or read from a file without passing all preceding records in the file. Individual records (transactions) can be processed as they are generated, to meet a user's immediate information requirements. There is no need to collect records into reasonable-sized batches beforehand (although this may be done in some systems, for efficiency or convenience). There is no need to make certain that records are arranged in a specific order as is required for sequential processing of records against punched-card or magnetic-tape master files.

The **manual input symbol** (⬠) represents data entered from manually operated online equipment. Examples are data generated from the operation of keyboards, light pens, console switch settings, badge readers, and the like. Here a human operator controls the rate of data entry and thereby directly affects the speed at which the job is processed.

The **online storage symbol** (▭) represents data held in intermediate, or temporary, storage on an external storage device. In general, this symbol is used for a device of the type required for random-access processing. As a group, these devices are referred to as **direct-access storage devices (DASDs)**. Magnetic disk storage units, magnetic drum storage units, and some very large mass storage subsystems are examples of direct-access storage devices. For some of these devices, the ANSI flowcharting standard also includes more specialized input/output symbols as alternatives. The specialized input/output symbols should be used wherever precise specification of input or output is required.

The display symbol is familiar to you. Its appearance in Figure 12-1 indicates that responses to inquiries are provided as output on any of a wide variety of display devices.

The **communication link symbol** (⅂) represents transmittal of data from one location to another by means of a transmission medium such as wires, cables, or

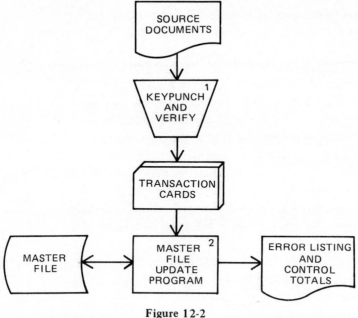

Figure 12-2

microwave radio circuits. When the direction of data flow is not obvious, arrowheads should be used with this symbol to indicate flow direction.

The system in Figure 12-1 is, in effect, a one-program system. It operates in an online-processing environment, as such systems often do. (Recall the discussion of such systems at the beginning of Lesson 11.) The system would be of little value, however, if the master stock file that it uses were not always current. This system assumes that, at the time the stock status program is executed, the master stock file contains the latest available stock status information.

To keep the master stock file up to date, another system is needed. This system performs master file updating. A very basic system for updating a master file used in random-access processing is shown in Figure 12-2. In step 1, data from source documents is keypunched and verified. This step is similar to the first step when processing data in a system that uses sequential processing techniques. The second step in the system is the file maintenance run. In this final step, the master file on online storage is updated. An error listing and control totals are also provided as output.

Unlike a magnetic-tape system, there is no old master file when a file on a DASD is updated. The concept of a "turnaround file" does not apply to updating of this type. Only the master records actually affected by the transaction records provided as input are read into computer storage. Each of these records is located directly by means of its **address** on the DASD. The complete master file is not rewritten. Unchanged records remain as they were. Updated records are rewritten in their original positions on the master file.

When a file is stored on a device such as a tape drive or a card reader, the records in the file can be organized in only one way: sequentially. On a DASD, there are a number of possible file organizations. Three of the most common are **sequential**, **direct**, and **indexed sequential**. Sequential files on DASDs are comparable to sequential files on magnetic-tape drives. Records can only be read in the sequence in which they are stored on the data-recording medium. An advantage of DASDs here is that data can generally be read from or written to DASDs faster than it can be read from or written to magnetic-tape drives. Therefore, although some business data-processing applications, for example, payroll and governmental reporting systems, use sequential processing techniques, the master files in the systems are stored on DASDs.

When direct organization is used, records are not written to the file in chronological sequence. Instead, the position of a record is determined by the address calculated for it in any one of a variety of ways.

As an example, one field of every record in the file may be identified as a **key field** (in much the same way that a control field is established for records in a sequential file). A series of instructions called a **randomizing routine** may be developed to operate on the content of the key field of any record to be stored and determine from it the address of the location on the DASD where the record should be placed. Assume the key field of the record contains a six-digit part number and that the randomizing routine uses the **division/remainder method** of address determination. The part number is first divided by the prime number closest to, but less than, the number of DASD **tracks** allotted to the file. The remainder of this division gives the relative track location for the record. This figure is then converted to an actual address on the DASD.

The indexed sequential organization is designed to allow both sequential and random processing. The records are stored on the DASD in sequence according to a key field, but one or more **indexes** are kept so that any record can be read randomly by first looking up its location in the indexes. After the location of the record on the DASD has been determined, the read/write head and data-recording medium positioning capabilities of the DASD are used to go directly to that location to read the record into computer storage for processing.

Although transaction records for random updates do not have to be in the same order as the records in the master file they are used to update, processing is more efficient if they are. Now that we have some understanding of how the order may be determined, we are ready to look at a somewhat more complex system for DASD master file updating. Such a system is shown in Figure 12-3.

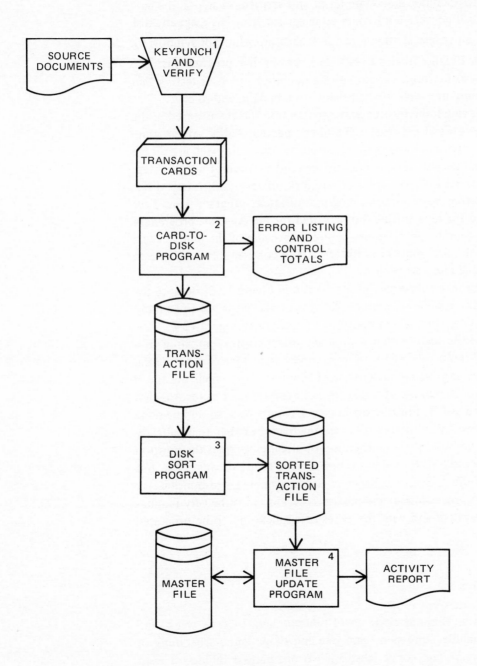

Figure 12-3

In step 1, the input transactions are keypunched and verified. In step 2, the data on the transaction cards is converted into data on magnetic disk. The **magnetic-disk symbol** (☐) used here is one of the more specialized input/output symbols for online storage mentioned earlier in this lesson. The **card-to-disk program** that performs the conversion also performs certain editing operations such as testing that numeric fields contain only numerals, that all fields contain data, and so on.

Step 3 is a sort step in which the records in the transaction file are arranged in the same sequence as the records in the master file to be updated. **A disk sort program** performs this function. One input file and one output file from this step are shown on the system flowchart, because that is the way we tend to think of the sort step. In common practice, several different areas of one disk, or several different disks, are used during disk sorting operations. Generally, a different program is used for disk sorting than is used for tape sorting, but as noted for the tape sort program in Lesson 11, this sort program is apt to be very complex. Because of the unique capabilities of DASDs, a disk sort program is likely to take considerably less time to execute than a comparable tape sort program.

Step 4 is a file maintenance run analogous to the run in Figure 12-2. Because the transaction records in this system are ordered, however, this run is apt to be more efficient than the file maintenance run in the system described in Figure 12-2.

As you might expect, the logic within a program that performs updating of a direct file or an indexed sequential file is more complex than that of a sequential file update program. The specific characteristics of the device on which the file is stored (number of cylinders, number of tracks per cylinder, number of records that will fit on one track, and so on) must be taken into account. What should be done when a record is supposed to be written on a certain track but that track already holds all the records it can? Or when another record already occupies the position calculated for a new record? Such details are beyond the scope of this book, but you should be aware of them. Systems designers and programmers responsible for file organization and file processing in random-access systems must be very familiar with the devices in the system and with the types of applications to be processed by it.

SAMPLE PROBLEM 12.1

Problem: Morgan General Hospital operates 24 hours a day, 7 days a week, 365 days a year. It must handle admission, care, feeding of patients; scheduling of patient rooms, operating rooms, x-ray labs, and so on; patient billing—of ever-increasing complexity because of a large variety of insurance plans, Medicare, and so on; employee payrolls; capital outlay; stock ordering and control; facilities maintenance; and other vital operations. It is difficult to imagine how Morgan General could manage its affairs without significant help from computers.

The systems analysis and design work needed to computerize operations at Morgan General is complex and extensive. To describe a single application area to the extent necessary to pursue design work is not possible in this book. We shall simply look at the design currently being proposed for a comprehensive system to deal with admissions, discharges, and financial transactions that pertain to hospital patients. Random-access processing techniques are used to read data from and write data to a patient master file and a bed master file. Since the files are online, the online storage symbol could be used to represent them on a system flowchart. The magnetic-disk symbol which identifies more precisely what type of device is used for storage, appears as an alternative in Figure 12-4. The **offline storage symbol** ($\triangledown$) is used to indicate that hard-copy documents and punched-card decks used for entry of data into the system are retained in the system for **backup** purposes. Though not immediately accessible to the computer during subsequent normal processing runs, they can be retrieved and re-processed if necessary to re-create lost or destroyed master-file data or other system outputs.

Solution: Input enters this system in the form of printed documents. Most of the types of input are readily identified by the words appearing on the system flowchart in Figure 12-4. "Corrections" refers to data previously submitted in error, detected in step 5 of a previous run, and corrected for re-input. "Setups" are additional input generated for each new patient.

On the basis of this input, three cards are created for each patient: a name and address card, an insurance-data card, and either an inpatient card or an outpatient card, indicating the age, sex, religion, race, and so on, of the patient. Data from the printed documents is punched into the cards, validated by an input edit program, and sorted into registration-number sequence as the various types of input are written to three different workfiles. Sorting is not mandatory because random-access processing is possible in this system, but the designers of the system suggest that sorting the records into registration-number order at this point will improve the efficiency of subsequent processing steps.

Techniques used to show the connection between parts of the system appearing on separate pages of the system flowchart are significant. A symbol representing both an output of one step and an input to a succeeding step is repeated if the succeeding step is on another page of the flowchart. A cross-reference to another appearance is given at the upper right of each symbol that appears repetitively.

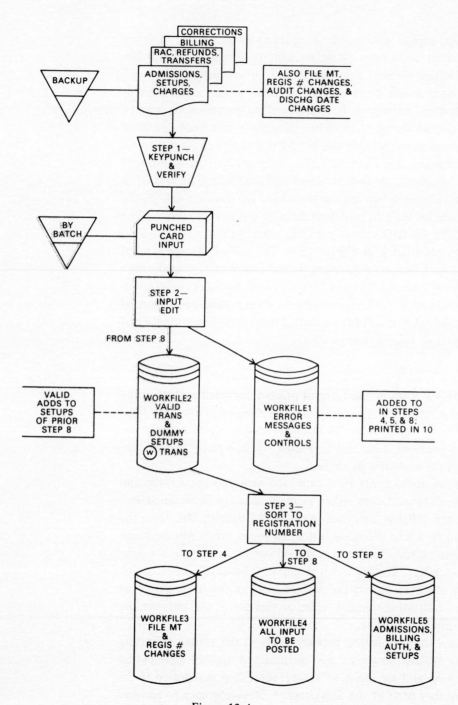

CORRECTIONS
BILLING
RAC, REFUNDS,
TRANSFERS
ADMISSIONS,
SETUPS,
CHARGES

BACKUP

ALSO FILE MT,
REGIS # CHANGES,
AUDIT CHANGES, &
DISCHG DATE
CHANGES

STEP 1—
KEYPUNCH
&
VERIFY

BY
BATCH

PUNCHED
CARD
INPUT

STEP 2—
INPUT
EDIT

FROM STEP 8

VALID
ADDS TO
SETUPS
OF PRIOR
STEP 8

WORKFILE2
VALID
TRANS
&
DUMMY
SETUPS
(W) TRANS

WORKFILE1
ERROR
MESSAGES
&
CONTROLS

ADDED TO
IN STEPS
4, 5, & 8;
PRINTED IN 10

STEP 3—
SORT TO
REGISTRATION
NUMBER

TO STEP 4

TO
STEP 8

TO STEP 5

WORKFILE3
FILE MT
&
REGIS #
CHANGES

WORKFILE4
ALL INPUT
TO BE
POSTED

WORKFILE5
ADMISSIONS,
BILLING
AUTH, &
SETUPS

Figure 12-4

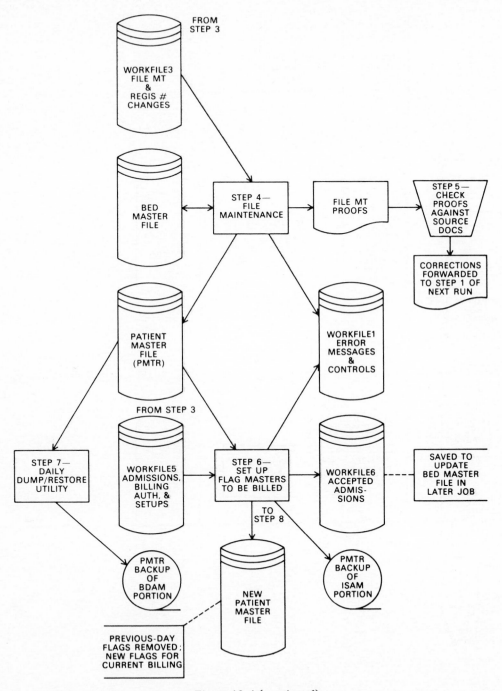

Figure 12-4 (continued)

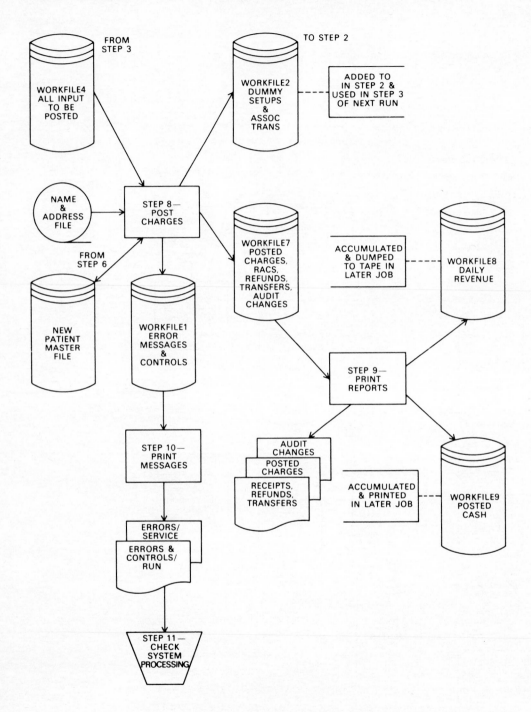

Figure 12-4 (continued)

Thus, for example, workfiles 3, 4, and 5 on page 1 of the system flowchart are shown again on pages 2, 3, and 2 respectively. This documentation is essential for persons who must read and understand the flowchart.

A great deal of information about the hospital accounting system is presented on this three-page system flowchart. Many more pages would probably be required to describe the system by a written narrative, and the description would be more difficult and less interesting to follow.

This sample problem is valuable not only because it demonstrates the use of flowcharting symbols and techniques but also because it points out a few of the considerations in system and program planning. A system design such as this one is the result of weeks or months of investigation, discussion, and study. Inputs and outputs of hospital operations, the best forms for data, the interrelationships of hospital functions, and the data flow within the hospital (system) must be determined. After the original system design has been established, specifications for programs within the system must be developed. Since eight computer programs are required to perform system processing, eight program flowcharts should supplement this system flowchart. Careful planning and construction of system and program flowcharts provides the basis for subsequent program coding, program and system testing, system implementation, and system or program modification. Such documentation helps to insure that required tasks will be accomplished as quickly and easily as possible.

exercises

1. (a) Distinguish between the following types of data-processing systems: offline, online, and real-time.
   (b) Describe a specific example of each of these system types.
2. Contrast random-access processing with sequential processing.
3. How does the updating of a master file on a DASD differ from the updating of a master file on magnetic tape?
4. Explain briefly the common types of organization used for files on DASDs.
5. Conventional keypunch devices have been used widely in business data processing environments for some time. They are now being replaced by key-to-tape devices and key-to-disk systems in environments where large volumes of data must be entered. The key-to-tape devices have keyboards for operator entry of data and provide magnetic tape on reels, cartridges, or cassettes as output. A key-to-disk system consists of from 8 to 64 keying devices from which data is entered and forwarded to a minicomputer. The minicomputer can perform data editing,

stores the edited data temporarily on magnetic disk, and then writes the correct records on magnetic tape for input to the main computer.

    (a) Modify the system flowchart in Figure 10-2 to provide for the use of a key-to-tape unit as the data-entry device. (If multiple key-to-tape units are used in a system, their outputs are generally pooled onto one tape by means of a pooling device provided with the units, for subsequent computer input.)

    (b) Modify the system flowchart in Figure 12-3 to provide for the use of a key-to-disk system to accomplish the data-entry function.

6. Study the system flowchart in Figure 12-4 to answer the following questions.

    (a) What is the form of the data as it initially enters the hospital accounting system?

    (b) In what other forms is data handled during system processing?

    (c) What manual operations are performed on data?

    (d) What master files does the system use?

    (e) Describe the handling of errors as shown on the system flowchart.

    (f) What provision is made for failure of the system during processing?

    (g) In which step is billing performed?

    (h) Identify all system outputs intended for direct reference by hospital personnel.

    (i) This system creates three data files for use by other hospital data-processing applications. What are they?

7. A list of typical data-processing functions is given below. Segments of system flowcharts follow. Indicate which flowchart segment corresponds to each description. (If you need to check the meanings of any of the symbols, refer to Appendix A.)

    (a) Data on cards is transcribed to magnetic tape in a card-to-tape run.

    (b) Data on source documents is keypunched in a manual operation to transcribe the data to punched cards.

    (c) The contents of a file in online storage are printed as output.

    (d) Data on magnetic tape is printed during an auxiliary operation.

    (e) Punched-card input is applied to update a magnetic-tape master file.

    (f) Output is provided to a display device at a remote location.

    (g) Input is extracted from a punched-card file retained in offline storage for use in a subsequent processing run.

    (h) Magnetic-tape input is used to update a master file on a magnetic drum storage device.

    (i) Input is provided manually from a cash register terminal at a remote location.

    (j) A printed document provided as output is placed in offline storage.

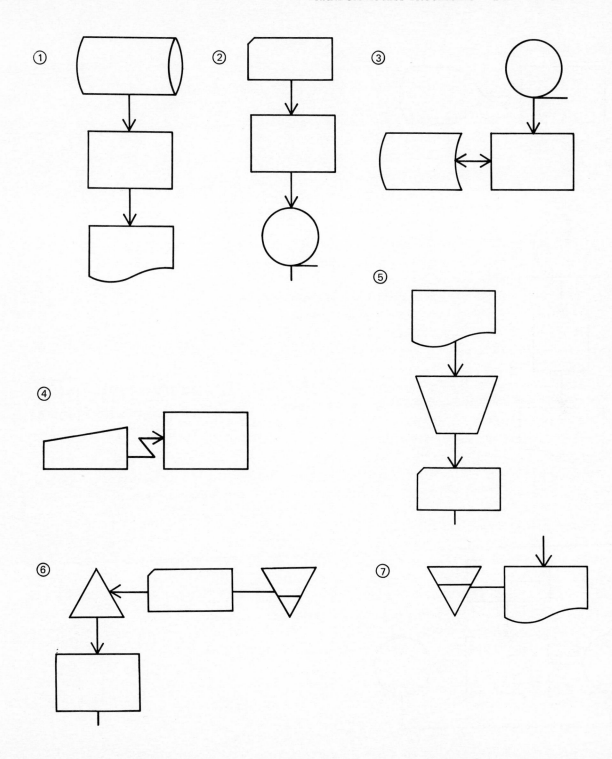

⑧

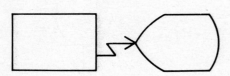

⑨

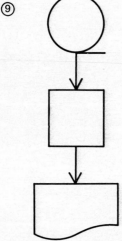

⑩

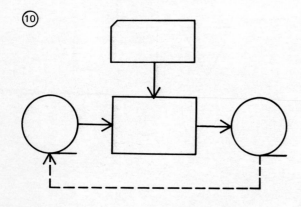

PLANNING THE SYSTEM STRUCTURE

Throughout the book, we have emphasized the use of basic control structures in program planning—the need to develop a solution algorithm that will lead to a well-structured program. We have seen how the inputs, outputs, and interrelationships of a set of programs, or system, can be depicted on a system flowchart. Though such a flowchart shows the *flow of work* within a system, it does not necessarily show the *flow of control*. In general, the two are equivalent only when both data and control pass from one program to the next, in a sequential manner, with no return of control to a previously executed program. In many systems, this is not the case. Therefore, it is difficult or impossible to tell from the system flowchart what actually happens during system processing.

Long complex programs were once marvelled at. Now, computer professionals, organizations that depend on computers, and individual users at terminals, all desire programs that are simple to understand and easy to use. They want programs that are easy to maintain when changes are required.

One approach to the problem of program complexity is to apply a **modular approach** to system and program development. We have already seen that a system may be composed of a single program or of several programs. In the same way, a program can be composed of one or more **modules**. Each module is a segment of logically related code that is part of the program. As much as possible, each module should be independent of all other modules. It should constitute a logical unit, performing one or a small number of functions of the overall problem-solving task. We saw one example of modular programming in Lesson 10: the read table routine (see Figures 10-3 and 10-4). Now it's time to explore modular design and programming techniques further.

To provide methodology, organization, and structure within a modular approach—and thus insure that the modules we define are functional units, and not just segments of code—we also apply a **top-down approach** to the development of a solution algorithm. This means that we identify first the major function to be accomplished, then we identify its subfunctions, their subfunctions, and so on, until we are satisfied that we fully understand the nature of the solution algorithm. The top-down design process (also called **structured design** or **composite design**) consists of a series of steps to define the functions required for the solution of a problem, in terms of the problem itself.

When using a top-down, modular approach, the systems designer or programmer plans the program or set of programs in **levels**. At each level, only the problem aspects relevant to that level are dealt with. The designer or programmer considers alternative ways to refine each part within the preceding level. He or she may take a look a level or two ahead if necessary to determine the best way to design at the present level. This process is repeated, continuing to successively lower levels of detail until all aspects of the solution algorithm have been defined. Programming details such as input/output headings, types of tests, and choices for variable names do not get in the way of critical design issues because they are considered only when it is appropriate to do so.

To document the design as it is formulated, the designer constructs one or more **structure charts,** or **hierarchy charts**. These charts are similar in appearance to a common business organization chart. An example is shown in Figure 13-1. We see here a structure chart for an accounts receivable system. The logical structure of the

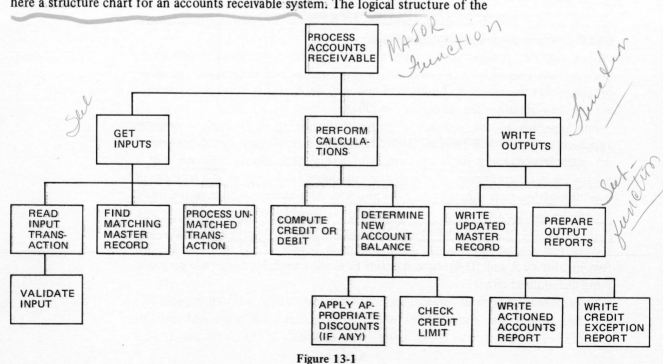

Figure 13-1

system is readily apparent. Each function or subfunction is described in terms of a verb (action) and an object (data affected): process accounts receivable, get inputs, and so on. As a design tool, the structure chart emphasizes structure and function, integral parts of the top-down, modular development process.

There is no single correct way to develop a structured design, just as there is no single correct way to draw a program flowchart. Look again at Figure 13-1. Given the same design task, another designer may have found it necessary to break the "Process Unmatched Transaction" function into subfunctions. Or, the design may have been structured so that the "Prepare Output Reports" function was not set up as a separate function, but instead was included in the report writing tasks (shown here as subfunctions).

One important principle of top-down, modular design that we mentioned above deserves special emphasis—as much as possible, each module in a program should be independent of all other modules. This means that each module shown on a structure chart of the program should begin execution only when control is passed to it from the module above it. Control must be returned to that higher module when the lower has completed its execution. One module must maintain overall control of activities, in much the same way that the president of a company provides overall direction and guidance for all the firm's employees. Major decisions should be made at as high a level in the hierarchy as possible. A lower-level module receives "orders" from its "boss" and then reports back the outcome of its actions. It may need to invoke one or more lower-level modules before it can report back, but whether or not it does so should not concern the boss. A module can send back some indication of results achieved or of conditions observed; on the basis of these, the higher module can decide what action to take. The lower-level module should not make decisions that its boss, or other modules at the same level or at higher levels, have to carry out.

Let's see how we might proceed in a top-down, modular fashion, given a well-defined statement of a problem to be solved. We shall use as our example the online inquiry application that we discussed briefly at the beginning of Lesson 12 (see Figure 12-1). Recall that this is a one-program system. A user enters a request for the current status of an item in inventory. This causes the determine stock status program to be executed. Its major function is to process that user request. A response is provided to the user, who can then take action accordingly.

A functional picture of the problem-solving requirements is sketched in Figure 13-2. It shows the sequence of functions that must occur in achieving the problem solution and the data passed from function to function. Note that, for this problem, the functional sequence takes the form of input functions, process functions, and output functions. This is the case for a large class of problems. It is the typical processing sequence that we have seen in many of our solution algorithms.

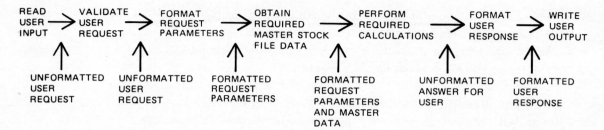

Figure 13-2

We have just completed step 1 of top-down, modular design:

1. Sketch a *functional picture* of the problem to be solved.

Now we are ready to do step 2:

2. Identify the *external, conceptual data streams*, both input and output.

This terminology may make this step sound awesome at first, but it need not be. "External" simply means outside of the system; "conceptual" means viewed independently of any particular input/output device. At this stage, we do not care whether the input device is a typewriterlike keyboard or a visual-display unit with a light pen attachment. We do not care whether the output is displayed on a screen or printed. All that is important is the data *content*—what input is coming to the program, and what output is to be provided from it. We see from Figure 13-2 that the input is the unformatted user request, and the output is the formatted response to the user.

Now we are ready for step 3:

3. Identify the *major* external, conceptual data streams (one for input and one for output) and determine their *points of highest abstraction*.

Since in our case we have only one input and one output, we do not have to determine which is major, or most important, in either case. The "point of highest abstraction" for an input stream means the point in the problem structure where the data is farthest removed from its physical input form, yet can still be viewed as coming in. It is the problem input data in its most abstract form—farthest removed from the input source. The "point of highest abstraction" for an output stream is the point in the functional picture where it first appears, that is, where it is farthest removed from the output device.

We add this information to the functional picture of the system (see Figure 13-3). The main processing function or functions of a program always fall between these

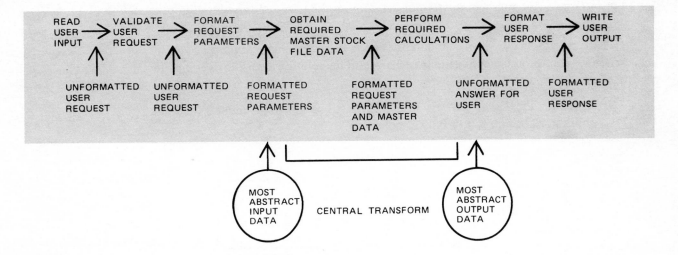

Figure 13-3

two points. This part of the program is called the **central transform** because it does the major data transformations within the solution algorithm.

At this point in the design process, it is time to describe the highest level structure for the solution algorithm in the form of a basic structure chart. So, step 4 is:

4. Construct a *basic structure chart.*

On this first, basic structure chart, we show:

- the primary input module (the function that gets the most abstract input data)
- the main processing module (the function that transforms the abstract input data to abstract output data)
- the primary output module (the function that puts the most abstract output data)
- the overall control module (the function that establishes the relationships between the three functions above)

Note that we are viewing "module" and "function" synonymously at this point. The functional picture that we have already constructed is very useful to us in formulating this equivalency (see Figure 13-4). From it, we extract the basic structure chart shown in Figure 13-5. This basic structure chart indicates that when the determine stock status program is executed, the overall control module, "Process User Request," will call "Receive User Input" when a terminal user enters a request,

"Prepare Response" to handle the request, and "Provide User Output" to send the response back to the user.

The final step in top-down, modular design is to repeat these design steps for all functions shown on the basic structure chart until the solution algorithm is complete. That is:

5. Reiterate the design process until all functions are fully defined (and the solution algorithm is thus fully established).

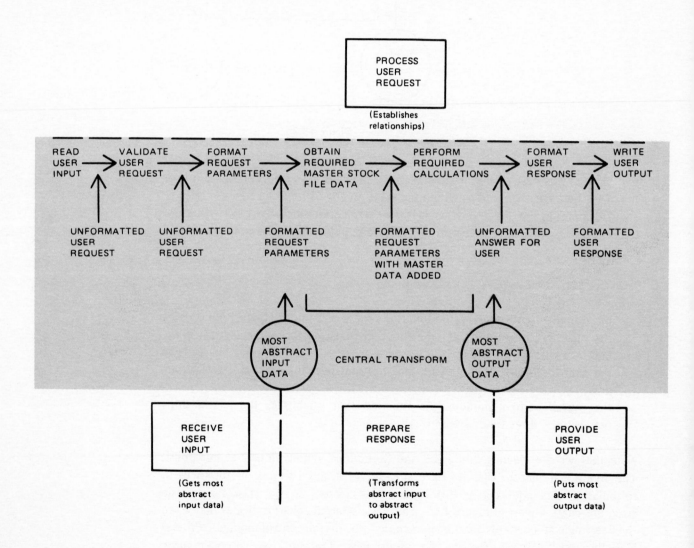

Figure 13-4

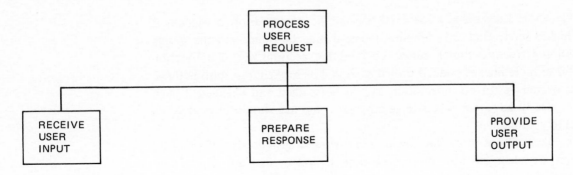

Figure 13-5

In completing this step, we refer to both the basic structure chart and the functional picture. Figure 13-6 shows the result: a structure chart for the "Determine Stock Status" program that includes all subfunctions.

You may be asking how one knows when to stop the top-down, modular development of a solution algorithm. To avoid program complexity, individual modules should be relatively small, but what does "relatively small" mean? Some designers state that a module may be any size up to that which fits in 4096 bytes of computer storage. Others propose that a module may be defined as the amount of code that one programmer can write and test during one month. This suggests a size of from 200 to 300 statements. Still others insist that each module should be no longer than 50 or 60 lines of code, the portion of a program that can be printed on a single page of the program listing.

In some cases, several very simple functions may be included in a single module.

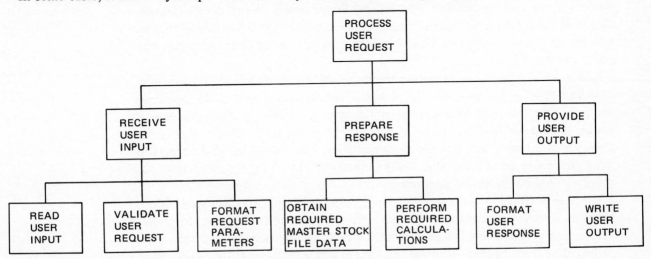

Figure 13-6

For example, short segments at a low level may be incorporated into a segment at the next higher level. That is, a minimal redesign may be done, and the design documentation (structure chart) should be modified accordingly. If a function requires 100 or more lines of code, it probably should be broken into subfunctions. Again, the overall design documentation should be studied and changed if such changes are clearly advisable. The size of a program module should ultimately be determined by its function.

Structure charts do not show the flow of work within a system—data flow, order of execution, or when and how often each module will be invoked. There is no order of execution implied by placing modules within a given level, or by arranging them in a left-to-right order beneath a higher-level module. It is essential not to try to read this information into a structure chart. The logic determining the control of the frequency and order of execution is inside the modules; it doesn't show on the chart. Structure charts show only the functions, their interrelationships, and the flow of control. Other forms of documentation created during the program development cycle are needed together with structure charts to complete the overall program documentation package. In general, any program created for repetitive use should be supported by: a functional description (extracted from the problem statement); the design documentation in flowchart, pseudocode, structure chart, or other design-language form; appropriate layout specifications; the program listing produced as one output of the translation process used to convert the programming-language statements to machine-language form; and operating instructions for the computer operator and/or a program user at a terminal.

How can the systems designer or programmer be sure that the design documentation will meet all the needs it must satisfy? Stated simply, design documentation should be created with the users of that documentation in mind. As a rule-of-thumb, you should explain a program design until the program coding itself and supporting comments can take over.

Each user of design documentation should be able to obtain exactly the information he or she seeks, no more and no less. Two common pitfalls in documenting are providing too little information, and providing too much. When developing design documentation, the systems designer or programmer should aim to be complete. Otherwise, not just the documentation but rather the whole programming effort may be of little value. On the other hand, providing too much information may obscure the critical portions.

There is a tendency for the programmer, especially one who has spent many hours at a task or is extremely familiar with the problem-solving area, to go too deeply into programming details. Providing a table of key variables and their uses, or including a list of these variables and their uses in a prologue at the beginning of code is often a wise approach. But mentioning insignificant variables, such as those used for intermediate storage of results, often confuses the reader. Difficult sections of code or potential trouble spots should be explained carefully. But commonplace data structures and trivial algorithms can be assumed to be understandable to the reader in their programming-language forms.

A major point well worth re-emphasizing is that design documentation and code must always agree. If the design changes, then the code must change. Conversely, if the code is changed, then the design documentation must be changed. Proponents of pseudocode point out that design documentation in pseudocode form can be entered as comments in the program itself or retained on a separate but readily accessible computer file. Once there, it can be updated easily with computer help whenever the program logic is changed. If program flowcharts are used as design tools, automated flowcharting techniques are especially valuable when frequent modifications to the program are required. Flowcharting programs have been developed by numerous software firms. For some of these, the programmer constructs a rough sketch of a flowchart, then describes the chart in a special flowcharting language acceptable as input to the flowcharting program. A printed flowchart is provided as output. Other flowcharting programs can accept the programming-language statements of a problem-solving program as input and provide a flowchart of the program logic as output, without any special action on the part of the programmer.

SAMPLE PROBLEM 13.1

Problem: Like so many business firms today, Eve's Toys, a manufacturer of puzzles, games, skateboards, flying saucers, and numerous other items for family leisure, faces a highly competitive marketplace. To produce high-quality products is not all that it takes for success; the company must also market them effectively. A comprehensive, detailed, and well-planned marketing strategy is of upmost importance to the company.

Although Eve's Toys uses an in-house computer system for its order writing, billing, accounts receivable, and inventory control applications, the company has not developed a computerized system for sales analysis. At this time, however, top-level management within the company recognizes that a key step in the development of a successful marketing strategy is the continual analysis of the current and past performance of the company's product line, its sales representatives, and its customers (the retail firms that sell the products).

The management of Eve's Toys believes that the sales data needed for sales analysis is already available in the company's master files, because it is essential to

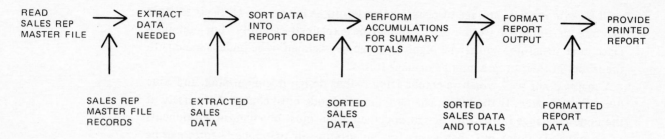

Figure 13-7

the company's basic business applications. What systems design and programming time would be required to develop a computerized system to extract and analyze this data for sales purposes?

Solution: Top-level management support for the development of a sales analysis system at Eve's Toys was demonstrated by the commitment of both personnel and funds to the background investigation, systems analysis, and design work needed. A group was formed to carry out the project, which was announced by a member of top-level management to further emphasize its importance.

After a brief but intensive study, the investigating group confirmed that data needed for sales analysis was indeed available within the company's master files.

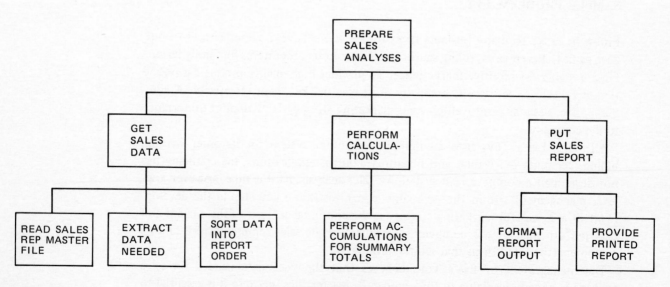

Figure 13-8

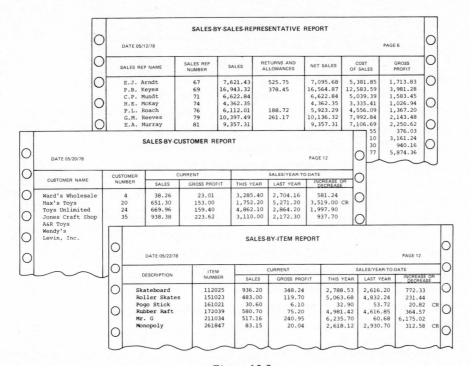

SALES-BY-SALES-REPRESENTATIVE REPORT

DATE 05/12/78   PAGE 6

SALES REP NAME	SALES REP NUMBER	SALES	RETURNS AND ALLOWANCES	NET SALES	COST OF SALES	GROSS PROFIT
E.J. Arndt	67	7,621.43	525.75	7,095.68	5,381.85	1,713.83
P.B. Keyes	69	16,943.32	378.45	16,564.87	12,583.59	3,981.28
C.P. Mundt	71	6,622.84		6,622.84	5,039.39	1,583.45
H.E. McKay	74	4,362.35		4,362.35	3,335.41	1,026.94
P.L. Roach	76	6,112.01	188.72	5,923.29	4,556.09	1,367.20
G.M. Reeves	79	10,397.49	261.17	10,136.32	7,992.84	2,143.48
E.A. Murray	81	9,357.31		9,357.31	7,106.69	2,250.62
	55					376.03
	10					3,161.24
	30					940.16
	77					5,874.36

SALES-BY-CUSTOMER REPORT

DATE 05/20/78   PAGE 12

CUSTOMER NAME	CUSTOMER NUMBER	CURRENT		SALES/YEAR-TO-DATE		
		SALES	GROSS PROFIT	THIS YEAR	LAST YEAR	INCREASE OR DECREASE
Ward's Wholesale	4	38.26	23.01	3,285.40	2,704.16	581.24
Max's Toys	20	651.30	153.00	1,752.20	5,271.20	3,519.00 CR
Toys Unlimited	24	669.96	159.40	4,862.10	2,864.20	1,997.90
Jones Craft Shop	35	938.38	223.62	3,110.00	2,172.30	937.70
A&R Toys						
Wendy's						
Levin, Inc.						

SALES-BY-ITEM REPORT

DATE 05/22/78   PAGE 12

DESCRIPTION	ITEM NUMBER	CURRENT		SALES/YEAR-TO-DATE		
		SALES	GROSS PROFIT	THIS YEAR	LAST YEAR	INCREASE OR DECREASE
Skateboard	112025	936.20	348.24	2,788.53	2,616.20	772.33
Roller Skates	151023	483.00	119.70	5,063.68	4,832.24	231.44
Pogo Stick	161021	30.60	6.10	32.90	53.72	20.82 CR
Rubber Raft	172039	580.70	75.20	4,981.42	4,616.85	364.57
Mr. G	211034	517.16	240.95	6,235.70	60.68	6,175.02
Monopoly	261847	83.15	20.04	2,618.12	2,930.70	312.58 CR

Figure 13-9

As an initial step, the group recommended that the billing/accounts receivable master file be used as a base for sales reporting.

In presenting their recommendations to management, the investigating group prepared the functional picture in Figure 13-7. This picture served as a basis for discussion of the systems design and programming time expected to be needed for completion of this initial part of the project. These functional steps were shown to be necessary in preparing each of three sales reports (with the exception that the sort function is not needed for the first one):

- Sales-by-Customer Report
- Sales-by-Item Report
- Sales-by-Sales-Representative Report

From this functional picture, the structure chart in Figure 13-8 was developed. Representative samples of the proposed reports were prepared and shown to top-level management for their approval (see Figure 13-9). Together, these design documents demonstrated the soundness of the group's proposal for the initial step in the development of a computerized sales analysis system. Additional personnel and funds were allocated so that the development of the system could proceed.

exercises

1. Distinguish between the information provided by a system flowchart and that provided on a structure chart.
2. Explain what a program module is. Be sure to identify its essential characteristics.
3. Discuss the relationships between a modular approach to program development and a top-down approach to a development effort.
4. Support or refute the statement, "The decision-making steps in a system should be made in the overall control module of the system if possible." In doing so, give two or more examples of program logic within a solution algorithm where decision making at a high level should (or should not) occur.
5. Refer to your response to Exercise 4. Regardless of the position you took, you will encounter valid exceptions. Give two or more examples of such exceptions.
6. Study Figures 13-2 through 13-6. Suppose that the master stock file is to be processed weekly to prepare a Slow-Moving Items Report (where "slow-moving" is defined to mean those items for which no orders have been filled during the past three months). Sketch figures analogous to Figures 13-2 through 13-6 to determine the functions and subfunctions required.

Use Figures 13-7 and 13-8 to complete Exercises 7 through 11.

7. What is the conceptual input data stream?
8. What is the conceptual output data stream?
9. What is the point of highest abstraction for input?
10. What is the point of highest abstraction for output?
11. What is the central transform?

12. Study the sales reports in Figure 13-9. Explain how a sales manager can use any one of these reports in formulating marketing strategy for the company.
13. Identify the various components that should be included in the overall documentation package for a system. Be sure to describe in detail the documentation needed for any one particular program within the system.
14. Collect representative documents of a system documentation package such as you described in response to Exercise 13, or create such a package for a system project that you are involved in.

USING HIPO

In the initial lessons in this book, we directed our attention primarily to a basic approach to problem solving. Since most of the problems that we discussed were relatively straightforward, we were able to develop solution algorithms (in either flowchart or pseudocode form) describing how relatively short, one-program systems should be implemented to solve the problems.

The solution algorithms developed in Lessons 9 and 10 used the same basic control structures as those we developed earlier. The program logic was somewhat more involved, however. We dealt with groups of data items as well as simple variables. We used subscripted variables to refer to specific elements of a group in list-processing and table-processing applications. In Lesson 10, we took our first look at a program consisting of more than one program module.

In Lessons 11 and 12, we looked at problem situations involving several programs instead of just one. We learned how to plan solution algorithms applicable in batch-processing and online-processing environments. We dealt with both sequential and random-access files.

The concept of *structure* is as important to understanding the flow of control in a system as it is to understanding and following the flow of control in a program. An effective way to develop structure is to apply a top-down, modular approach to both system and program development. As we saw in Lesson 13, the idea behind this approach is to design a program or set of programs in levels. First, we identify the major function or functions in the solution algorithm. Then we break those functions into subfunctions at a lower level in the solution hierarchy. We continue this breaking down, or decomposition, until all of the functional program modules needed to solve the problem have been identified.

A key to success in developing program modules that are truly independent of other modules in a program or system is to identify not only the functions but also all the inputs to and outputs from each function. In programming terminology, we say that the **interfaces** to each function must be defined. In general, the systems designer or programmer should employ data coupling but avoid data interconnection. Under **data coupling**, all inputs to and outputs from a module are passed as data elements, to or from that module. A **data interconnection** exists when a module depends on or alters variables outside its boundaries. Dependencies—and difficulties—often arise when a module refers to **global** (inter-module) variables or accepts input data directly from an I/O device. The I/O portion of a program is, by definition, the portion of the program that interfaces with the outside world; it is therefore most subject to change. Generally, I/O processing should be concentrated in a few, short, specially selected modules apart from the rest of the program.

A program design and documentation tool developed to emphasize not only structure and function, but also the inputs and outputs to each function is **HIPO diagramming**. *HIPO* is an acronym for *H*ierarchy plus *I*nput-*P*rocess-*O*utput. A typical HIPO package contains the three types of diagrams outlined in Figure 14-1. These are:

- **Visual table of contents**. This diagram looks much like the structure charts we discussed in Lesson 13 but it carries additional information. The names and identification numbers of all succeeding diagrams in the HIPO package and their relationships are shown in a hierarchical, graphic form. A **legend** in the lower left portion of the diagram tells what the various symbols used in the HIPO package mean. With this visual table of contents, a user of the package can locate readily a particular level of information or a specific diagram without thumbing through the entire package.

- **Overview diagrams**. These high-level diagrams describe in general terms the inputs, processes, and outputs of high-level, major functions. Each diagram is divided into *input, process,* and *output* parts, with arrows used as symbols to show the relationships between the inputs, process steps, and outputs depicted in these parts. An overview diagram refers the user to detail diagrams that expand the general functional description by providing additional information.

- **Detail diagrams**. These lower-level diagrams describe specific functions in specific terms. Graphically, they are similar to overview diagrams, but the type of information given is different. Whereas an overview diagram may identify a particular file that is processed as input, a detail diagram gives a functional description of particular items in the file, or their names, or both. A detail diagram breaks a function down into the smallest details needed to understand it. An *extended description* area of the diagram is used to amplify the process steps shown on the diagram, as needed. It may contain statement labels, routine names, and other specific references to the module code. The number of levels of detail required to develop a solution algorithm fully depends in large part on the factors that must be considered within the problem to be solved.

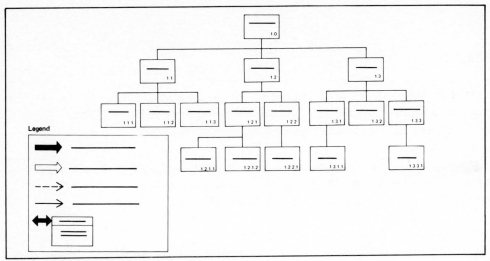

(a) Visual Table of Contents

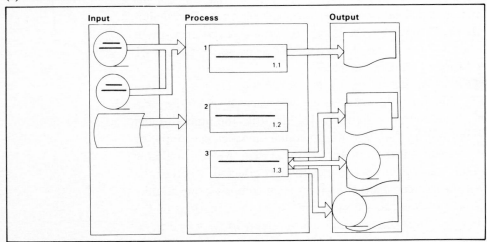

(b) Overview Diagram

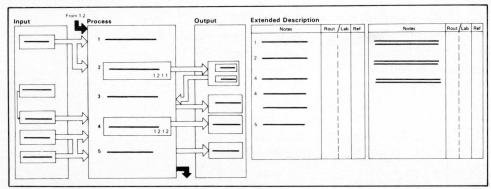

(c) Detail Diagram

Figure 14-1

SAMPLE PROBLEM 14.1

Whether we are engaged in the data-processing operations of a company, or simply work for a company in another capacity, we count on receiving a paycheck for what we do. So there is at least one business data-processing application of more than casual interest to us—payroll processing.

In simplest terms, the inputs to a typical payroll application are employee time cards. The outputs are employee paychecks. The processing consists of the basic arithmetic operations needed to figure out how much employees should be paid (see Figure 14-2).

Of course, the problem isn't really that simple. The computer can't perform calculations on payroll data until the data has been read into computer storage. An employee time card tells the number of hours the employee worked, but not the employee's pay rate, or how much tax should be withheld, or what other deductions are to be made. If the computer were simply to write a paycheck without making any record of having done so, at the end of the year, none of the wage statistics required for W-2 forms would be available.

A more detailed, precise description of payroll processing is given in the system flowchart in Figure 14-3. This system flowchart is useful because it shows the computer programs needed in the payroll system. It also identifies the inputs to and outputs from each program, and the data-recording medium on which each input or output is stored. It doesn't document the structure of the system. We can't tell how the flow of control within the system during execution is effected, whether the required programs are well-structured, whether each program comprises one module or several modules, and so on. Nor can we determine what the functions of the modules are, if there are some. In short, we can't tell by simply looking at the system flowchart whether or not a top-down, modular approach to system and program design has been carried out.

Alternative, or supplementary, design documents showing the payroll system structure are given in Figure 14-4. These structure charts group the processing functions within the payroll system into three systems (or subsystems). The first two subsystems (page 168) prepare the inputs for the third subsystem (page 169).

Figure 14-2

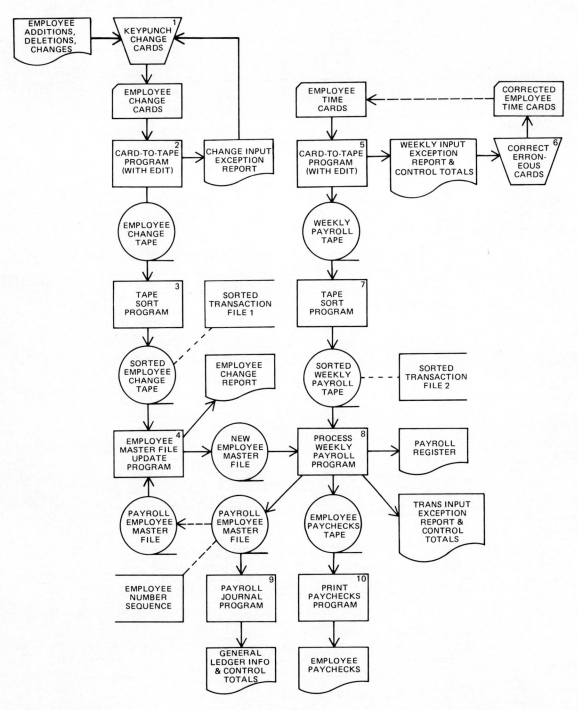

Figure 14-3

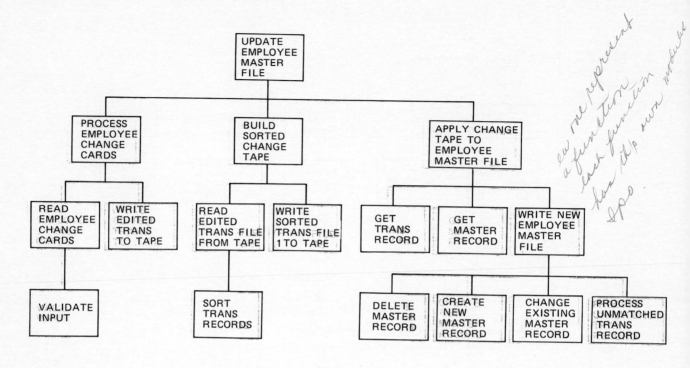

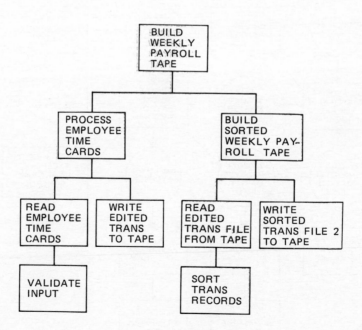

Figure 14-4

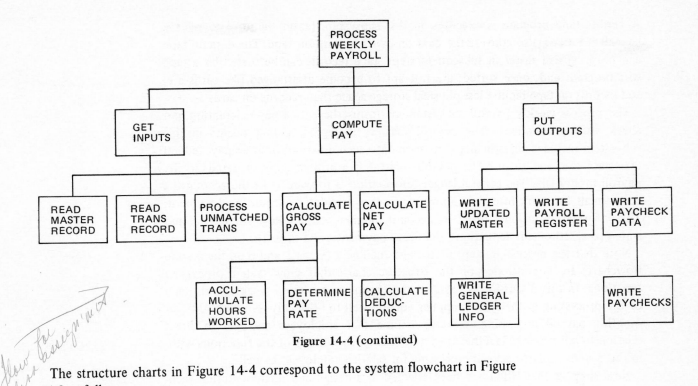

Figure 14-4 (continued)

The structure charts in Figure 14-4 correspond to the system flowchart in Figure 14-3 as follows:

- Update employee master file (includes steps 2, 3, and 4 as shown on the system flowchart)
- Build weekly payroll tape (includes steps 5 and 7 on the flowchart)
- Process weekly payroll (includes steps 8, 9, and 10)

Before the end of a pay period, the accounting department of the company obtains data on new employees, employees who have left the company, and recent changes that must be made to master file records for existing employees. Typical changes include increase or decrease in number of tax exemptions, different marital status, department transfer, new address, different work code, and adding or deleting certain voluntary deductions. These changes are processed within the update employee master file subsystem. The employee master file created as one output of the last run of the process weekly payroll subsystem is used as a second input to this subsystem, and a new (updated) employee master file is provided as output for use in the next process weekly payroll subsystem run.

The build weekly payroll tape subsystem processes the employee time cards submitted by employees to indicate how much they've worked during the week.

A card-to-tape program is executed in this subsystem (as in the process weekly payroll subsystem) to convert the data on cards to data on tape. The data on tape can be processed faster in subsequent steps; tape records can be sorted by a tape sort program and, once sorted, are not apt to become disarranged like cards are; and records on tape require less physical storage space than records on cards.

The process weekly payroll subsystem performs the actual pay calculation and check writing functions. The payroll master file updating that occurs in this subsystem includes adjustments to year-to-date accumulations of gross pay, federal tax, state tax, and so on. The payroll register is a printed copy of details in the payroll master file. The general ledger information is forwarded to the accounting department for entry into the company's final consolidated accounting document. This information includes totals by account number, withholdings for federal and state taxes, retirement deductions, sick leave payments, and so forth.

Note that the processing steps performed manually (steps 1 and 6 on the system flowchart) are not included on the structure charts that show system processing functions. In this discussion we assume the payroll is processed weekly, but much of the processing in the system applies equally well to bi-weekly, semi-monthly, or monthly payroll processing. We also assume that employees are paid in direct relation to hours worked (rather than a flat salary), but many of the functions within the system apply to payroll processing for salaried employees as well.

Now suppose that HIPO had been selected as a design and documentation technique to be used in planning the payroll system. In this case, instead of the structure charts shown in Figure 14-4, the systems designer or programmer creates a HIPO package for each of the payroll subsystems. For example, let us direct our attention to the HIPO package for the third subsystem, process weekly payroll.

Compare the HIPO visual table of contents to the third structure chart in Figure 14-4. They are very similar. The subsystem structure remains the same. It is represented by a hierarchical, treelike diagram in both. Each rectangular symbol on the visual table of contents refers to another diagram in the HIPO package. The name and identification number of the diagram are given inside the symbol. For example, Diagram 1.1, "Get Inputs," further describes the input function of the highest-level function of this HIPO package. The highest-level function is itself described by Diagram 1.0, "Process Weekly Payroll."

If the identification numbers on a visual table of contents are chosen appropriately, they support the visual representation of the vertical relationships of functions along each path, or **branch**, of the structural hierarchy. For example, the leftmost branch in Figure 14-5 includes **nodes** at levels 1.0, 1.n, and 1.n.n. The visual table of contents also shows horizontal relationships. For example, level 1.n comprises nodes 1.1, 1.2, and 1.3.

We see that the process weekly payroll function, or subsystem, has an overall control module by that name, documented on Diagram 1.0. Its subfunctions accomplish the tasks we've learned to look for in a system: input, processing, and output. Each of these subfunctions breaks down into subfunctions at one or two lower levels in the solution hierarchy.

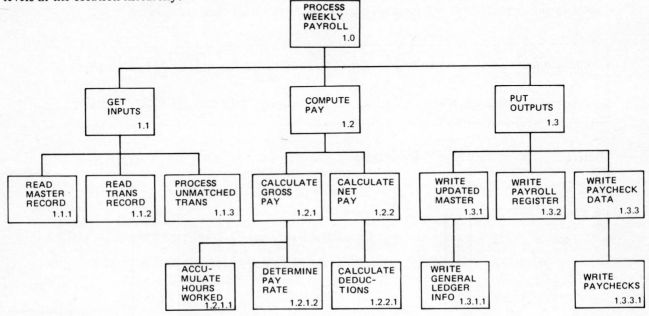

Legend

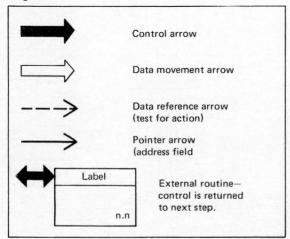

(solid black arrow)	Control arrow
(hollow arrow)	Data movement arrow
(dashed arrow)	Data reference arrow (test for action)
(thin arrow)	Pointer arrow (address field
(double-headed arrow with Label box n.n)	External routine—control is returned to next step.

Figure 14-5

Figure 14-6 shows a typical overview diagram—in this case, Diagram 1.0 of our example. The purpose of this overview diagram is to give us *general* knowledge of the process weekly payroll function. The heading at the top of the diagram provides important administrative and identification information about this function. The standard flowcharting symbols for data-recording media are used to represent the inputs to and outputs from the function because all of them are obtained from or

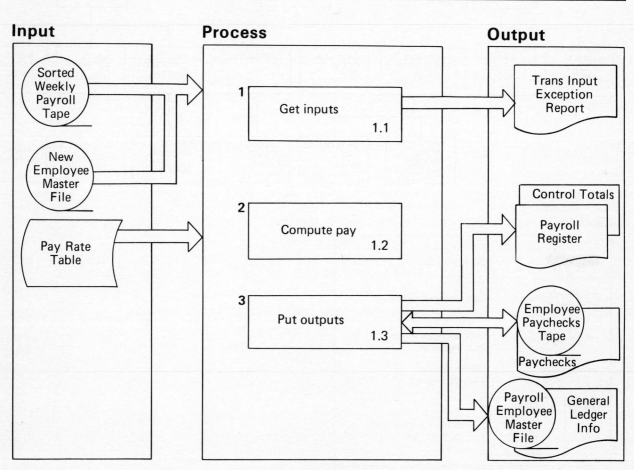

Figure 14-6

written to external input/output devices (rather than manipulated in computer storage). **A data movement arrow** extends (1) from a flowcharting symbol to the processing step in which data is read, or (2) from a processing step to the flowcharting symbol for the media on which data is written. Since the employee paychecks tape is written to in processing step 3, and also read from in that step, a double-headed data movement arrow connects the symbol for this tape and step 3 on the diagram.

All of the processing steps on the overview diagram in Figure 14-6 are enclosed in boxes. This means that the steps are explained in greater detail on lower-level diagrams. The number in the lower right-hand corner of each box is the number of the next lower-level diagram that further describes the particular processing step. The three diagrams referred to on this overview diagram describe the functional modules at level 1.n of the structural hierarchy depicted on the visual table of contents (Figure 14-5).

Figure 14-7 shows a typical detail diagram—in this case, Diagram 1.2.1 of our example. We can tell from the visual table of contents that the "Compute Pay" subfunction (Diagram 1.2) breaks into two subfunctions: "Calculate Gross Pay" (Diagram 1.2.1) and "Calculate Net Pay" (Diagram 1.2.2). It is the first of these two subfunctions that is shown.

A detail diagram has a heading, just as an overview diagram does. The input, process, and output parts in the upper half of the diagram are called the **chart portion** of the diagram. The lower half of the diagram is called the **note portion**. Both must be present on a detail diagram. The chart portion is also required on an overview diagram, but the note portion may be omitted (as it has been, in our examples thus far) if no additional information at the particular level being diagrammed is required.

The **control arrow** and text "From 1.2" near the top of the process part of Diagram 1.2.1 indicate that control is passed to this calculate gross pay module from the module described in Diagram 1.2. By referring to the visual table of contents in Figure 14-5, we can verify that this is "Compute Pay," the module directly above it in the structural hierarchy (as it should be, in a well-structured program). The control arrow and text "Return" at the bottom of the process part of Diagram 1.2.1 indicate that control is returned to the calling module, compute pay, after all processing steps mentioned on this diagram are executed (once again, this is as it should be).

The inputs to Diagram 1.2.1 (Calculate Gross Pay) shown in Figure 14-7 are already available in computer storage when execution of the module is initiated. Therefore, they are shown by boxes representing internal storage areas, rather than by standard flowcharting symbols for input/output. (If external input/output devices were referenced, however, it would be appropriate to use the standard flow-

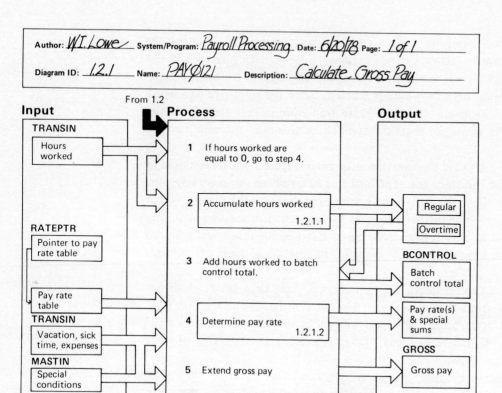

Author: *W.I. Lowe* System/Program: *Payroll Processing* Date: *6/20/78* Page: *1 of 1*

Diagram ID: *1.2.1* Name: *PAY0121* Description: *Calculate Gross Pay*

From 1.2

Input

TRANSIN
Hours worked

RATEPTR
Pointer to pay rate table

Pay rate table

TRANSIN
Vacation, sick time, expenses

MASTIN
Special conditions

Process

1 If hours worked are equal to 0, go to step 4.

2 Accumulate hours worked
   1.2.1.1

3 Add hours worked to batch control total.

4 Determine pay rate
   1.2.1.2

5 Extend gross pay

Output

Regular
Overtime

BCONTROL
Batch control total

Pay rate(s) & special sums

GROSS
Gross pay

Return

Extended Description

Notes	Rout / Lab	Ref
1. No accumulations needed; special conditions apply.	PAY01212	1212
2. Calculate separate totals for regular hours and overtime hours.		1211
4. Work code is search key for pay rate table.	WK CD	1212
4. Check for overtime pay, shift pay; allow for vacation time, sick time, holidays; check for commissions.		1212
5. Check for expense payments.	PEXP	

Notes	Rout / Lab	Ref

Figure 14-7

charting symbols here just as on overview diagrams.) The label actually used for a storage area or a particular field of an area should be indicated if one has been assigned. This label should be printed in capital letters. In contrast, text describing a data item or data group should not be written in all capital letters. Generally, it is convenient to write the label above the box for the item and the descriptive text inside the box. There are several examples of this technique in Figure 14-7.

As Figure 14-7 indicates, all that we have just said about inputs applies to the representation of outputs as well. Note also that in either case, the size of a box has no significance. Each box can be as large as necessary to enclose the text needed to describe the data represented by it.

One of the inputs to the calculate gross pay module is a data pointer, RATEPTR. The **pointer arrow** from RATEPTR to the box representing the pay rate table indicates that this pointer is used to access the pay rate table. We can also tell from this diagram that the pay rate table is used in step 4. Steps 2 and 4 of the functional process description are enclosed in boxes. We can refer to Diagrams 1.2.1.1 and 1.2.1.2 to learn more about how hours worked are accumulated and pay rates determined, respectively. (Looking again at Figure 14-5, we might expect this to be the case.) Steps 1, 3, and 5 are not enclosed in boxes. This means that they are performed by the calculate gross pay module without enlisting the help of lower-level modules.

The extended description area contains numbered notes corresponding directly to some of the numbered processing steps in the process part of the upper portion of the HIPO diagram. A note is included for a processing step whenever further explanation of that step is needed at this level in the solution hierarchy. Thus, the note for step 1 indicates what happens if the input value for hours worked is equal to 0. The routine label PAY01212 is given in the "Rout/Lab" column, and a reference to the appropriate HIPO diagram, 1.2.1.2, is given in the "Ref" column. The extended description area may also refer to non-HIPO documentation such as flowcharts or pseudocode expressing particularly complicated logic, layout specifications for input and output, and so forth. It must not be assumed that information in a column carries forward until a new entry is encountered in the column. If the same entry applies in consecutive steps, it should be indicated repetitively, as is the reference to 1.2.1.2 in Figure 14-7.

Standards for the representation of types of data, types of usage, and other program-design considerations have been proposed for HIPO. These and other guidelines are documented in the IBM Corporation manual, *HIPO—A Design Aid and Documentation Technique*. IBM has also developed a HIPO template and HIPO worksheets.[1] (The HIPO template is similar to the flowcharting templates described

---

1. The IBM order number for the HIPO manual is GC20-1851. The template and worksheet have order numbers GX20-1971 and GX20-1970 respectively.

in Lesson 4. If a HIPO template is not available, a flowcharting template can be used to construct many of the symbols used on HIPO diagrams.)

It is clear from this example that HIPO is well suited to the top-down, modular approach to program development. A HIPO package does an excellent job of handling the requirements of a variety of people who rely on system and program documentation for different purposes. A manager, for example, wants an overview of the system. This is readily obtainable from the visual table of contents and overview diagrams. A programmer responsible for implementing the design needs documentation at a very detailed level for programming purposes. Personnel responsible for isolating, identifying, and fixing errors, or for making changes to an existing program to provide for functional changes in the problem to be solved, require documentation that points quickly from function to code.

An important point to remember when constructing HIPO diagrams is that they show function, not detailed internal program organization and logic. Detail diagrams are guides to the writing or interpretation of program coding, not replacements for it. If additional development or documentation of internal program logic is needed, program flowcharts and pseudocode are valuable tools that help programmers to see all aspects of a problem, and to organize their thoughts more fully.

Because HIPO supports a top-down, modular approach, it helps the systems designer or programmer to incorporate structure within a solution algorithm. The major functions at upper levels in a solution hierarchy contain the control logic of the program or set of programs being developed. They determine when and in what order lower-level functions are to be executed. The corresponding portion of a highlevel-language program, for example, will consist primarily of CALL statements, PERFORM statements, DO loops, and IF-THEN-ELSE control structures. The lower-level functions are the workers; here, simple statements to be executed sequentially will predominate. The structured programming control structures emphasized in this book enact the top-down, modular approach at its lowest level— individual programming-language statements. Systems designers and programmers who are familiar with the tools described in this book are well equipped to develop correct, effective problem solutions. The programming-language representations of these solution algorithms will be well-structured programs.

exercises

1. (a) What does the acronym *HIPO* stand for?
   (b) Why is this acronym appropriate?
2. List and explain the three types of diagrams included in a HIPO package. Be sure to distinguish clearly between them.

Refer to Figure 14-3 to answer Exercises 3 through 10.

3. What master files are used in the system?
4. Explain what transaction files are used in the system, and how they are used.
5. What manual operations are required?
6. In what steps is editing of input performed?
7. What are the inputs to the system?
8. What are its outputs?
9. Tell as much as you can about the employee master file on the basis of the system flowchart.
10. What happens in step 7? Why is this step advisable?

Refer to Figure 14-4 to answer Exercises 11 through 14.

11. What modules may be called into execution by the process employee change cards module?
12. What modules may be executed during processing to write a new employee master file?
13. What module writes information to be included in the company's general ledger for annual reporting purposes?
14. What module must be called during execution of the module that calculates net pay?
15. (a) Look again at Exercises 3 through 10. Which of these exercises can you do by referring to Figure 14-4?
    (b) Look again at Exercises 11 through 14. Which of these exercises can you do by referring to Figure 14-3?
    (c) On the basis of your work in response to (a) and (b) above, what conclusions can you draw?

Refer to the HIPO documentation in Figures 14-5 through 14-7 to answer Exercises 16 through 24.

16. How many modules are included in the process weekly payroll subsystem?
17. What is the overall control module of the system?
18. (a) Sketch and identify the four types of arrows that may be used in HIPO documentation.
    (b) Describe a processing situation where use of each of these arrows would be appropriate.
19. What are the outputs of the put outputs module?
20. What lower-level modules may be called into execution during execution of the put outputs module?
21. What processing steps are actually performed by the calculate gross pay module?

22. (a) What causes the calculate gross pay module to be executed?
    (b) What happens when execution of this module is completed?
23. What routine determines whether any reimbursements for expenses are due to an employee?
24. What field of an employee transaction record is used as a search key when accessing the pay rate table to determine what pay rate should be applied in calculating gross pay?

25. Create a **HIPO** package for a system project that you are involved in, as suggested by your instructor or in your on-the-job environment.

SYSTEM FLOWCHARTING SYMBOLS

American National Standards Institute (ANSI) recommendations for use of symbols on system flowcharts are presented in this appendix. The shape of each recommended symbol, its meaning, and one or more examples are given. The symbols that you are most apt to find useful in your design work are explained in greater detail in one or more lessons in this book. The lesson in which each symbol is introduced is given in parentheses following the explanation of the symbol.

Input/Output Symbol

Generalized input/output function; data available for processing (input) or the result of processing (output) (Lesson 2)

Process Symbol

Any processing function; an operation or group of operations; usually, a computer program (Lesson 2)

Flowline Symbol

Direction of data flow; normal flow is from top to bottom and from left to right; if otherwise, arrowheads are required on flowlines (Lesson 2)

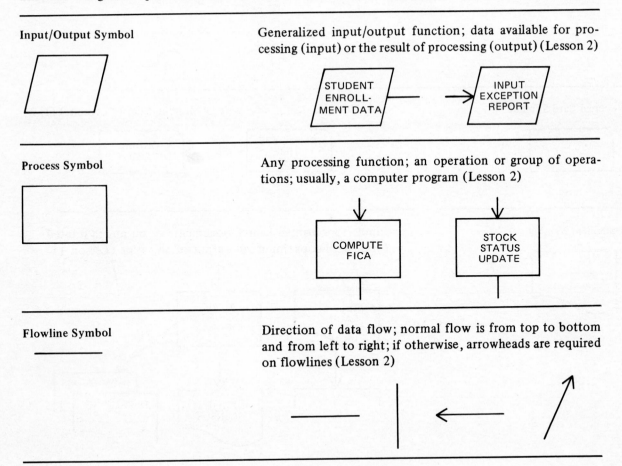

Annotation Symbol

Additional explanation; comments (Lesson 11)

```
        PREBILLING        TO CUSTOMER-
          SORT    - - - -   NUMBER
                           SEQUENCE
```

Connector Symbol

Exit to, or entry from, another part of the flowchart; if the corresponding connector appears on another page, a page reference should be included

TO PAGE 5

(A2)   (D3)—

Punched-Card Symbol

Input/output using any type of punched card (Lesson 11)

```
  EMPLOYEE              ORDER
    TIME        →       CARDS
   CARDS
```

Document Symbol

Input from printed source documents or output in printed form; hard-copy input or output of any type (Lesson 11)

```
  BILLS OF            ALPHA
  LADING             REPORTS
                     PROGRAM

                                    ADMISSIONS

                     INPATIENT      DISCHARGES
                      CENSUS
```

Display Symbol

Any kind of transitory data not in hard-copy form or intermediate output data used during the course of processing to control processing; usually, output displayed at time of processing by means of online printer-keyboards, visual-display units, plotters, and so forth (Lesson 11)

Magnetic-Tape Symbol

Input/output using any type of magnetic tape (Lesson 11)

Punched-Tape Symbol

Input/output using any type of punched continuous material, such as paper tape, punched plastic tape, punched metal tape, and the like; the medium must be an indefinite length, and the data must be represented by punched patterns

Manual-Input Symbol

Input entered manually at time of processing by means of online keyboards, console switches, and so forth (Lesson 12)

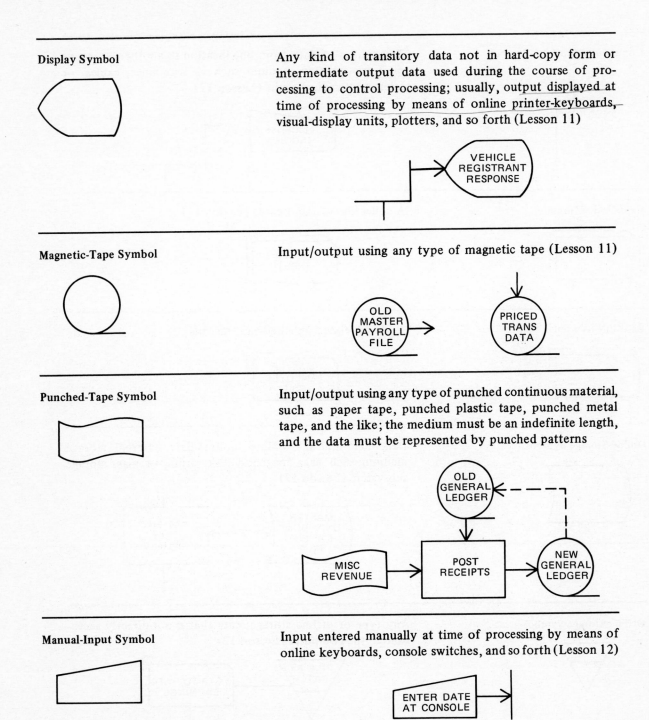

Communication-Link Symbol

Transmittal of data from one location to another by means of a transmission medium such as wire lines, cables, or microwave radio circuits (Lesson 12)

LICENSE INQUIRY

Card Deck Symbol

A collection of input cards (Lesson 11)

DEPT 3 INPUT

Card-File Symbol

A file of related punched-card records

MASTER EMPLOYEE FILE

Online-Storage Symbol

Data held on any online intermediate external storage medium such as a magnetic disk, drum, or mass storage subsystem (Lesson 12)

MASTER UNIV HOSP PATIENT FILE

PATIENT FILE UPDATE

Offline-Storage Symbol

Any type of offline storage; data that is not directly accessible to the computer (Lesson 12)

FILE BY BATCH

YEAR-TO-DATE EARNINGS

Magnetic-Disk Symbol

Data stored on a disk device of any type, especially a magnetic disk (Lesson 12)

MASTER NAME FILE

Magnetic-Drum Symbol

Data stored on a drum device, especially a magnetic drum (Lesson 12)

ACCNTS PAYABLE WORKFILE

Core-Storage Symbol

Data stored in a magnetic core or similar high-speed device other than the primary storage unit of the computer

TABLE OF LOGS

Manual-Operation Symbol

Process performed manually or using equipment that operates at the speed of a human operator (Lesson 11)

ACCTS REC PROOFS

PROVE ACCT TOTALS

Auxiliary-Operation Symbol

Process using equipment not under direct control of the primary computer at an installation and not limited to the speed of a human operator (Lesson 12)

MAINT REPORT TAPE

TAPE-TO-PRINT CONV

TYPE I MAINT REPORT

PROGRAM FLOWCHARTING SYMBOLS

American National Standards Institute (ANSI) recommendations for use of symbols on program flowcharts are presented in this appendix. The shape of each recommended symbol, its meaning, and one or more examples are given. The symbols that you are most apt to find useful in your design work are explained in greater detail in one or more lessons in this book. The lesson in which each symbol is introduced is given in parentheses following the explanation of the symbol below.

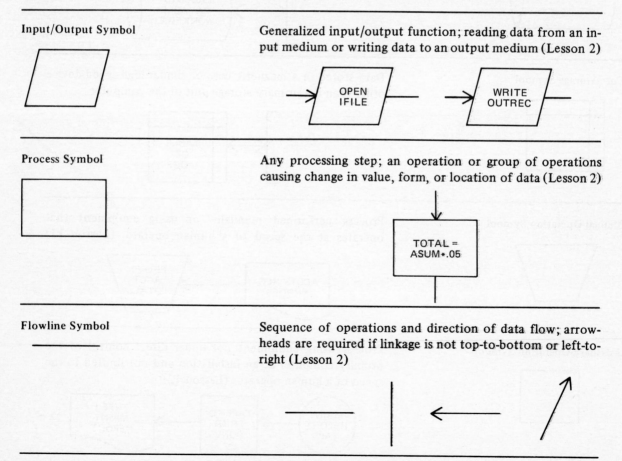

Input/Output Symbol

Generalized input/output function; reading data from an input medium or writing data to an output medium (Lesson 2)

OPEN IFILE

WRITE OUTREC

Process Symbol

Any processing step; an operation or group of operations causing change in value, form, or location of data (Lesson 2)

TOTAL = ASUM*.05

Flowline Symbol

Sequence of operations and direction of data flow; arrowheads are required if linkage is not top-to-bottom or left-to-right (Lesson 2)

Annotation Symbol

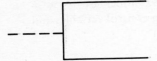

Additional explanation; comments (Lesson 5)

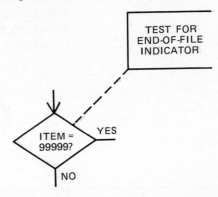

Connector Symbol

Exit to, or entry from, another part of the flowchart; if the *to* or *from* step is on another page, a page reference should be stated (Lesson 3)

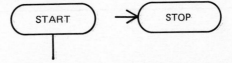

Terminal, Interrupt Symbol

Terminal point in a flowchart—start, stop, or break in the line of flow (Lesson 2)

Decision Symbol

Decision-making operation, usually based on a comparison, that determines which of two or more alternative paths should be followed (Lesson 3)

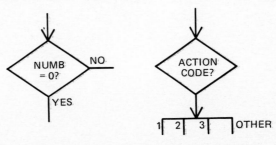

Preparation Symbol

An operation performed on the program itself for control, initialization, overhead, or cleanup; examples are to set a switch, to place a limit value in a loop control variable, and to initialize an accumulator (Lesson 4)

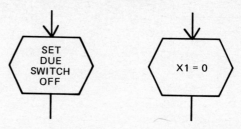

Predefined Process Symbol

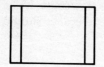

One or more operations specified in detail elsewhere, such as in a reference manual or on a different flowchart, but not on another part of the flowchart where this symbol appears (Lesson 5)

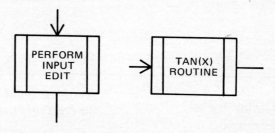

STRUCTURED-PROGRAMMING CONTROL STRUCTURES

The three basic patterns of structured programming—SIMPLE SEQUENCE, IFTHENELSE, and DOWHILE—are summarized in this appendix. Two additional control structures, CASE and DOUNTIL, which represent frequently used combinations of these basic patterns, are also summarized. First, the general form of the control structure is given. Then an example is expressed in both flowchart and pseudocode forms. The lesson in which each structure is introduced is given in parentheses following the explanation.

SIMPLE SEQUENCE

the execution of one processing step after another, in normal execution sequence (Lesson 2)

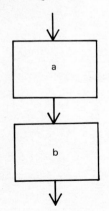

```
Function a
Function b
```

Example:

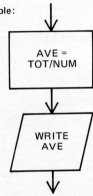

Find average $\left(\dfrac{\text{accumulated total}}{\text{number of items}}\right)$

Write average

IFTHENELSE   the selection of one of two alternatives (Lesson 3)

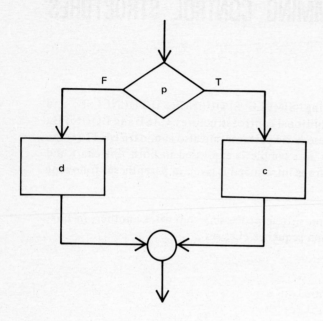

```
IF p THEN c ELSE d
```

Example:

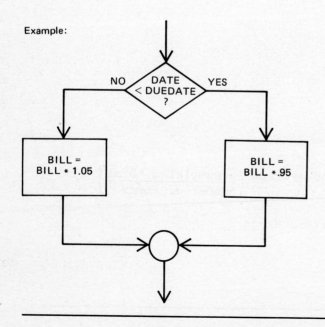

```
IF date is less than due date THEN

    apply 5% discount to bill

ELSE

    apply 5% interest to bill

ENDIF
```

DOWHILE

the execution of processing steps within a program loop, as long as a specified condition is true; a leading-decision loop (Lesson 4)

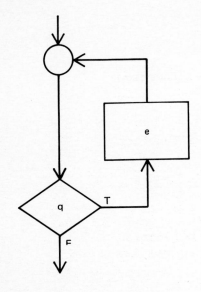

DO e WHILE q

Example:

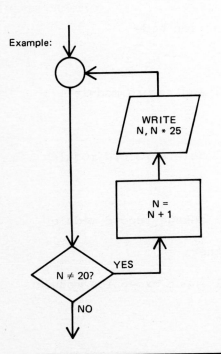

DOWHILE counter N is not equal to 20

    Add 1 to N

    Write N, N*25

ENDDO

CASE

the selection of one of more than two alternatives (Lesson 5)

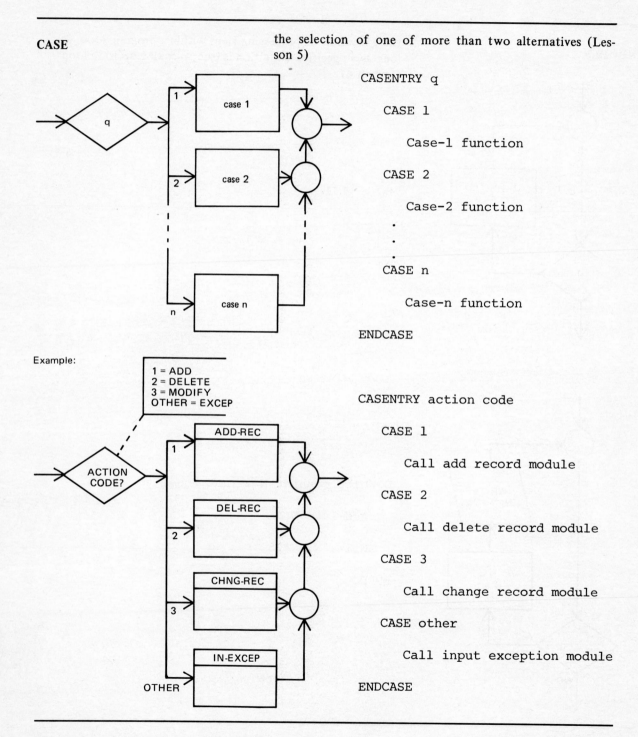

```
CASENTRY q

    CASE 1

        Case-1 function

    CASE 2

        Case-2 function
                    .
                    .
                    .
    CASE n

        Case-n function

ENDCASE
```

Example:

```
CASENTRY action code

    CASE 1

        Call add record module

    CASE 2

        Call delete record module

    CASE 3

        Call change record module

    CASE other

        Call input exception module

ENDCASE
```

DOUNTIL

the execution of processing steps within a program loop, until a specified condition is true; a trailing-decision loop (Lesson 6)

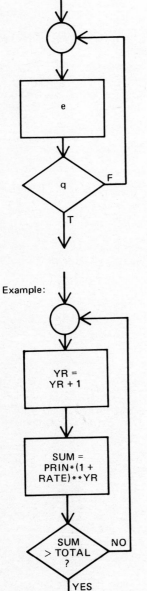

Example:

```
DO e UNTIL q
```

```
DOUNTIL sum of principal and interest (SUM)

   is greater than limit value (TOTAL)

   Add 1 to number of years

   SUM = principal * (1 + rate) ** years

ENDDO
```

RESPONSES TO SELECTED EXERCISES

Responses to selected exercises from each of the lessons in this book are given in this appendix. For some of these exercises, there is no one correct answer. In such cases, the responses are representative answers to the problems.

lesson 1

1. An algorithm is an ordered set of operations, from a given set of basic operations, that produces the solution to a problem in a finite number of steps.
3. Whether or not a haircut is required.
5. (a) Have keys?
7. Reads the newspaper

9.

lesson 2

1. (a) A data-processing system consists of the methods and devices used to perform a series of planned actions and operations upon data to achieve a desired result.

3.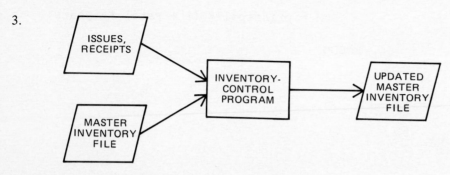

5. (a) From top to bottom and from left to right
7. Your flowchart should show SIMPLE SEQUENCE, the straightforward execution of one processing step after another.

lesson 3

1. A decision-making step provides for a choice among alternative paths, a variation in processing sequence dependent on the data entering the system or situations that arise during processing.
3. (b) is the correct response.
5. (a)

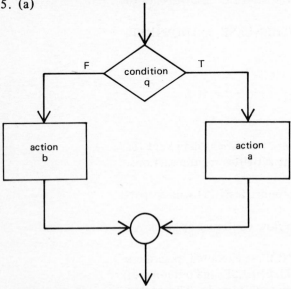

7. The connector symbol acts as a collector, emphasizing that the IFTHENELSE has only one entry point and one exit point.
9. The customer who returns more than 10 cases receives 50 cents more per case than he or she would have if less than 10 cases had been returned.

lesson 4

1. A program loop permits a sequence of processing steps to be done repetitively (that is, re-executed, or reused) during processing.
3. (a)

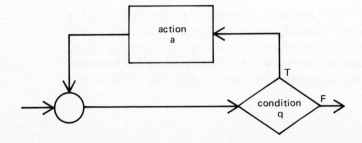

5. Since each of the basic patterns has only one entry point and one exit point, it can be treated as a SIMPLE SEQUENCE pattern. Further, a series of these basic patterns can be treated as a SIMPLE SEQUENCE. (We say that the contained patterns are nested.) The combining of patterns and building up of logic can continue until a complete program is constructed. A program containing only basic patterns, and combinations of them, can have only one entry point and one exit point. It can itself be thought of as a SIMPLE SEQUENCE, or basic building block.

7. The three basic patterns are SIMPLE SEQUENCE, IFTHENELSE, and DOWHILE.

9. See flowchart, page 195.

lesson 5

1. (a) A master file contains a large volume of relatively permanent data kept for reference purposes. A detail file contains current activities, or transactions, to be processed against a master file.

3. For adjustments, which are code 4 transactions, the most tests (5) will be performed.

5. For transactions with code 1, 2, 3, or 4, the program flow continues at block A1 on page 5 of the flowchart.

7. All decision-making steps within a SIMPLE SEQUENCE are executed, regardless of the outcomes of any of the tests. In a nested IFTHENELSE, the outcome of each test determines whether or not a succeeding test is made. The nested IFTHENELSE control structure may be exited without executing some of the decision-making steps.

9. The solution algorithm implies that division is expected to be the most frequently required operation, multiplication the next most frequent, and so on, with fewest inputs of the "other" category.

lesson 6

1. (a) A leading-decision loop

3. There are various ways to provide "general-purposeness," or flexibility. One is to read the number of values to be added, as the first input value, and assign it to a loop control variable, say N. Another is to continue reading input values until a special end-of-file indicator is encountered. Your algorithm for Exercises 2 and 3 should use one of these approaches or a similar one that accomplishes the same objectives.

7. See flowchart, page 196.

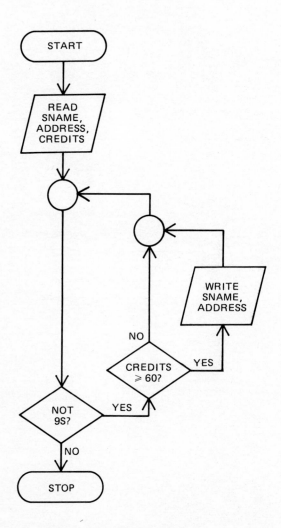

RESPONSE 4-9

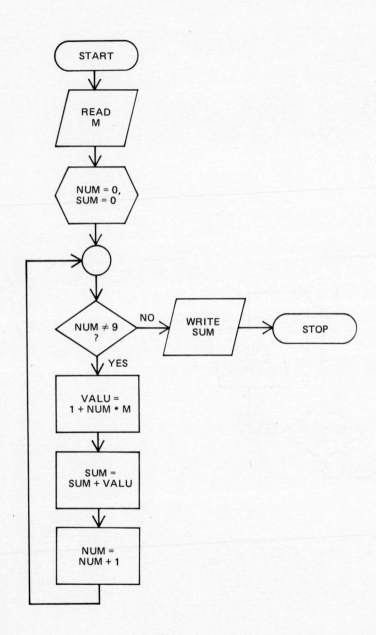

RESPONSE 6-7

lesson 7

1.
```
Start
Read A, B, C, D
Assign A to Q
IF Q is greater than B THEN
   assign B to Q
(ELSE)
ENDIF
IF Q is greater than C THEN
   assign C to Q
(ELSE)
ENDIF
IF Q is greater than D THEN
   assign D to Q
(ELSE)
ENDIF
Write Q
Stop
```

3. (a) Your table of storage locations should look like the table in Figure 7-2. Your table of input values should be similar to the table in Figure 7-3, but contain the values 25, 330, .35, and 102.

7. See flowchart, page 198.

lesson 8

1. A coder is given the design documentation of a solution algorithm; it serves as a guide as the coder writes (codes) the algorithm in a programming-language form. A programmer's responsibilities are broader; he or she participates in the creation and documentation of the program design as well as in program coding, check-out, and completion of documentation.

3. Re-verification of design documentation is necessary if changes are made to the solution algorithm during program coding, say to adapt to the particular computer or programming language in use. If any changes are made to the solution algorithm during program checkout, the design documentation must be changed and re-verified.

7. (a)

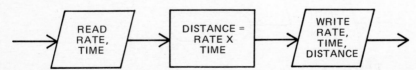

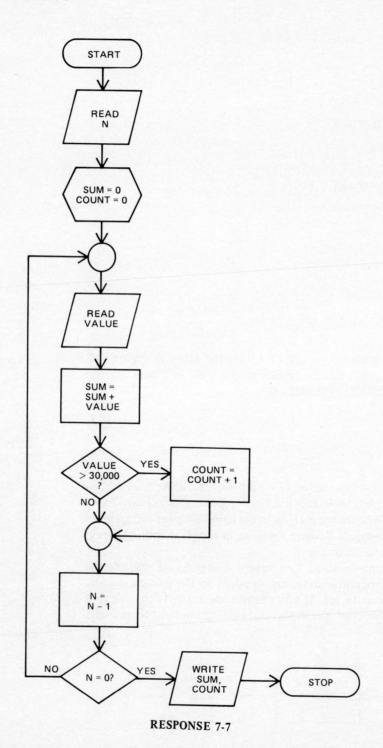

RESPONSE 7-7

lesson 9

1. (a) A data group is a collection of similar data items for which a single storage area large enough for all the items is reserved. The individual items are not assigned names; instead one name is assigned to the entire group of items.
3. (a) E(4) contains 48.
7. (a) 708   52   10   .091

lesson 10

1. (a) A table-lookup operation is a search of the entries in a table to find a table entry applicable to the value being processed against the table.
3. (a) A routine is a sequence of instructions that performs a specific function, or functions; a subroutine is a generalized sequence of instructions that performs a specific function and can be included in other subroutines, routines, or modules of a program; a module is a logical program unit that can be developed separately from other program units, then combined with them to form a complete, executable program.
7. The office code read as input and assigned to INCOD is the search key.

lesson 11

3. Records are often stored in files on punched cards or magnetic tape in business data processing systems. Records on either of these media must be processed sequentially—that is, in the order in which they are stored. So that processing can be done efficiently, the records are normally written on the file in a specific order or arranged (sorted) into a specific order before they are used in processing. For the same reason, input records to be applied against such a file are normally sorted into the same order as the records in the file before they are used in processing.

lesson 12

3. When a master file on a DASD is updated, only the master records actually affected by the current input are read into storage, changed, and rewritten as output; unaffected records are not processed. When a master file on magnetic tape is updated, all of the records on the tape are read and then rewritten to tape, whether or not they must be changed. When a master file on a DASD is updated, individual records are rewritten back to their original places on the same master file; there is no old master because the old records are destroyed by

the rewrite operation. When a master file on tape is updated, an old master remains and a new master is created during the update run. Magnetic-tape files must be processed and updated sequentially, whereas sequential, random, or a combination of sequential and random processing may be used with files on DASDs.

lesson 13

7. The conceptual input stream consists of sales representative master file records.
9. The point of highest abstraction for the input occurs after it has been extracted and sorted but before it is used in subsequent processing.
11. The central transform is the perform accumulations for summary totals function.

lesson 14

7. The inputs to the system are (1) employee additions, deletions, and changes, and (2) employee time cards.
9. The employee master file is a sequential file of records stored in employee-number sequence on magnetic tape. Changes to basic employee data in the file are made by the employee master file update program, which provides the new (updated) employee master file as output. This file is then used as input to a process weekly payroll program. The program provides a payroll employee master file as output, which is really the employee master file with current payroll data added. This file is used as the input employee master file (still called the payroll employee master file) for the next run of the employee master file update program.
11. The read employee change cards module and the write edited transactions to tape module may be called by the process employee change cards module.